MILESTONES

Joseph Cardinal Ratzinger

MILESTONES

Memoirs 1927–1977

TRANSLATED FROM THE GERMAN

BY

Erasmo Leiva-Merikakis

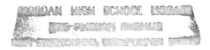
IGNATIUS PRESS   SAN FRANCISCO

Title of the German edition:
Aus meinem Leben: Erinnerungen (1927–1977)
© 1998 Deutsche Verlags-Anstalt, Stuttgart

Title of the Italian edition:
La mia vita: Ricordi (1927–1977)
© 1997 Edizioni San Paolo, Milan

Rights to reproduce photographs
granted by Edizioni San Paolo

Contents

I

Childhood between the Inn
and the Salzach Rivers

It is not at all easy to say what my hometown really is. As a rural policeman, my father was transferred frequently, so we were continually on the road. In 1937, however, when my father turned sixty and retired, we moved into the house in Hufschlag, outside Traunstein, and for the first time we had a real home. But even our previous moves occurred within a limited radius—in the triangle formed on two sides by the Inn and the Salzach rivers, whose landscape and history marked my youth. This had been an ancient land worked by the Celts, which then became a part of the Roman province of Raetia and always remained proud of its twofold cultural roots. Celtic artifacts have been discovered that point to a very ancient past and connect us with the Celtic world of Gaul and Britain. There are still fragments of Roman roads, and many places can refer to their former Latin names with pride in a longer history. Roman soldiers doubtless brought Christianity into the region already in pre-Constantinian times, and, even if the faith was largely buried in the chaos of the migration of peoples, streamlets of it were nonetheless able to continue flowing through this dark epoch, to be revitalized by the missionaries who afterward arrived from Gaul, Ireland, and England. Some experts even posit the existence of Byzantine influences. Salzburg (Roman *Juvavum*) became a Christian metropolis that strongly determined the cultural history of this land down to the Napoleonic era. Virgil, the remarkably obstinate and rebellious bishop from Ireland, was a decisive personality, and even more so was Rupert, a native of Gaul, who is venerated here in a livelier way than Corbinian, the founder of the bishopric of Freising. This is explained by the fact that only after the Napoleonic Wars was the Bavarian portion of this land joined to the newly founded archbishopric of Munich-Freising. And, in speaking of this part of our ancient Christian history, we must not forget the Anglo-Saxon Boniface, who gave the whole of what was then Bavaria its ecclesial structure.

I was born on Holy Saturday, April 16, 1927, in Marktl am Inn. The fact that my day of birth was the last day of Holy Week and the eve of Easter has always been noted in our family history. This was connected with the fact that I was baptized immediately on the morning of the day I was born with the water that had just been blessed. (At that time the solemn Easter Vigil was celebrated on the morning of Holy Saturday.) To be the first person baptized with the new water was seen as a significant act of Providence. I have always been filled with thanksgiving for having had my life immersed in this way in the Easter mystery, since this could only be a sign of blessing. To be sure, it was not Easter Sunday but Holy Saturday, but, the more I reflect on it, the more this seems to be fitting for the nature of our human life: we are still awaiting Easter; we are not yet standing in the full light but walking toward it full of trust.

Since we left Marktl in 1929, barely two years after my birth, I have no real memory of it, only the stories of my parents and of my brother and sister. They have told me of the deep snow and teeth-clattering cold that reigned on the day of my birth. My two older siblings to their great chagrin could not come to my christening because of the danger of catching cold. The time the family spent in Marktl was not an easy one: unemployment was rife; war reparations weighed heavily on the German economy; battles among the political parties set people against one another; endless illnesses visited the family. But there were also many beautiful memories of friendship and neighborly aid, memories of small family celebrations and of church life. And I must not forget to note that Marktl is very close to Altötting, the venerable and ancient Marian shrine dating from the Carolingian era, which since the late Middle Ages has become the great pilgrimage site for Bavaria and western Austria. Just in those years Altötting received new renown with the beatification and then the canonization of Brother Konrad of Parzham (1818–1894), a Capuchin who had been porter of his monastery. In this humble and thoroughly kind man we saw what is best in our people embodied and led by faith to its most beautiful possibilities. I have often reflected since then on this remarkable disposition of Providence: that, in this century of progress and faith in science, the Church should have found herself represented most clearly in very simple people, in a Bernadette of Lourdes, for instance, or even in a Brother Konrad, who hardly seemed to be touched by the currents of the time. Is this a sign that the Church has lost her power to shape culture and can take root only outside the real current of history? Or is it a sign that the clear view of the essential, which is so often lacking in the "wise and prudent" (see Mt 11:25), is given in our days, too, to little ones? I do think that precisely these "little" saints are a great sign to our time, a sign that moves me ever more deeply, the more I live with and in our time.

But back to my childhood. The second stop on our journey was Tittmoning, the small town on the Salzach River whose bridge constitutes the border with Austria. With an architecture heavily marked by the Salzburg style, Tittmoning remains my childhood's land of dreams. There is the big, even majestic, town square with its noble fountain, bordered by the Laufen and Burghausen Gates, surrounded by the proud old houses of burghers—truly a square that would do great honor to bigger cities. Above all, the shop windows illuminated at night during the Christmas season have remained in my memory like a wonderful promise. It was in Tittmoning that Bartholomew Holzhauser wrote down his apocalyptic visions at the time of the Thirty Years' War. But his greatest merit was to have picked up and revived the idea (going back to Eusebius of Vercelli and Saint Augustine) of having secular priests live together in community. The religious house, or *Stift*, that he founded in this small city on the Salzach left behind certain titles: the pastor was called *Stiftsdekan* ("dean of the *Stift*"), and the parochial vicars were called "canons". As was the custom in canonry churches, the Blessed Sacrament was reserved in a separate chapel and not in the tabernacle on the high altar. All of this gave us the feeling that our little city in every respect had something special about it. This could also be seen in the fact that the rectory was enthroned like a small castle on an elevation high above the town. Most of all, however, we loved the beautiful old Baroque monastic church that had once belonged to the Augustinian canons and was now lovingly looked after by the English Sisters. The girls' school and the kindergarten (then called "children's establishment") were now housed in the old monastic buildings. What my memory recalls most sharply is the "Holy Sepulcher", with many flowers and colorful lights, that would be set up in this church between

Good Friday and Easter and that, before any rational comprehension, brought home the mystery of death and resurrection to both my exterior and interior senses. But this is far from doing justice to all the special features that made our town so lovely and us so proud of it. When you climb to the top of the hill that rises over the valley of the Salzach, you come to the Ponlach Chapel, a lovely Baroque shrine completely surrounded by woods. Near it you can hear the clear waters of the Ponlach rushing down to the valley. We three children would often make a little pilgrimage with our dear mother to this spot and allow the peace of the place to have its effect on us. And then, of course, there is the unforgettable mighty fortress that towers over the town and tells its story of past grandeur. The police station—and hence our living quarters—occupied the most beautiful house on the town square, a house that had formerly belonged to the chapter of the *Stift*. It is true that the beauty of the façades concealed living spaces with little comfort to speak of. The paving on the floor was full of cracks, the stairs were steep, the rooms crooked. The kitchen and the living room were narrow, and the bedroom by contrast had been the chapter room, which did not exactly make for comfort. For us children, all of this meant mystery and excitement, but for Mother, on whom the burden of housework rested, all of this meant a great deal of hardship. So she was all the happier when she could go out with us on long hikes. We liked to cross over to nearby Austria. There was a special feeling in going "to a foreign country" by just taking a few steps, although in this country they spoke the same language as ours and, with a few small differences, even the same dialect. In the fields in the fall we looked for wild lettuce, and by the Salzach in the meadows Mother showed us how to find many useful things for our nativity scene, of which we were particularly fond. One of my most delightful memories is the visit we would make around Christmas time to an elderly lady whose nativity scene almost filled the whole of her living room and had so many wonderful things that you could not contemplate it long enough. I also remember the attic where a friend would stage his puppet theater for us, with figures that fired our imagination.

But we also sensed that our happy childhood world was not set in a paradise. Behind the beautiful façades much silent poverty lay concealed. Our small border town, left behind by progress, was harshly hit by the economic crisis. The political climate had visibly intensified. Although I did not concretely understand what was happening, I do remember the shrill campaign posters and the incessant rounds of elections they announced. The inability of the republic we had at that time to create political stability and hence engage in convincing political action became apparent even to a child in the turbulent clash of the parties. The Nazi Party gained ever stronger ascendancy by declaring itself the only alternative to the threatening chaos. When Hitler failed in his attempt to have himself elected president of the Reich, Father and Mother breathed a sigh of relief; but they did not exactly rejoice in the election of President Hindenburg either, since in him they did not see a reliable opponent to the rise of the brownshirts who dreamed of power. Time and again, in public meetings, Father had to take a position against the violence of the Nazis. We could very clearly sense the immense anxiety weighing him down, which he could not manage to shake even during ordinary activities.

2

First School Years in the Village—
The Shadow of the "Third Reich"

Father thus decided, toward the end of 1932, to change locations once more. In Tittmoning he had simply said too much against the brownshirts. In December, shortly before Christmas, we moved into our new home in Aschau am Inn, a well-to-do agricultural village consisting of large, imposing farms. Mother was pleasantly surprised by the lovely living quarters assigned to us. A farmer had built a country house that was modern by the standards of those days and rented it to the rural police. The offices and the apartment of the second-in-command were on the ground floor. We were assigned the second story, and there we found all the makings of a cozy home. A front garden with a lovely wayside cross belonged to the house, and also a big meadow with a carp pond in which I almost drowned once while playing. In the middle of the village, as is always the case in Bavaria, there was a large brewery whose restaurant was the meeting place for the men on Sundays. The actual village square was at the other end of the place, with yet another nice restaurant, a church, and a school.

We children naturally missed at first the wonderful things of the small city we had been so proud of. The neo-Gothic style of the lovely village church could not be compared with what we were used to in Tittmoning. The stores were plainer and the dialect a bit coarser, so that in the beginning there were many words we could not understand. But very soon we grew fond of our village and learned to appreciate its own beauty. The first thing to weigh heavily on us was the historical crisis of the times. We had arrived in December 1932, and already on January 30, 1933, Hindenburg transferred to Hitler the position of chancellor of the Reich, an event that in the language of the Party came immediately to be known as the "seizure of power"—and that is exactly what it was, too. From the first instant power was exercised. I myself have no memory of that rainy day, but my brother and sister have told me that the school had to perform a march through the village that, of course, soon turned into a tramp through the slush that could hardly have fired anyone's enthusiasm. Nevertheless, there already existed both open and secret Nazis in the village who now saw their hour arrive and, to the terror of many, were bringing their brown uniforms out of the trunk. The "Hitler Youth" and "League of German Girls" were introduced, and my brother and sister were obliged to participate in their activities. It mortified my father to have to work now for a government whose representatives he considered to be criminals, even if local policemen in the village were for the time being, thanks be to God, hardly affected by the changes. As far as I can see, the sole result of the new regime, during the four years we spent here, was the practice of spying and informing on priests who behaved as "enemies of the Reich". It goes without saying that my father had no part in this. On the contrary, he would warn and aid priests he knew were in danger.

It is clear that National Socialism could transform life in the little village only quite slowly. At first, for instance, the schoolteacher continued to be—as was the custom in Bavaria—the organist and choir director in the church as well, and he also continued to teach Bible class, while the catechism was the pastor's responsibility. At first it seemed that all of this had been assured anew by the concordat, but soon it became evident that contractual fidelity meant nothing to the new masters. The battle against parochial schools began to be waged. The still existing bond between school and Church was now to be dissolved, and the school's spiritual foundation was no longer to be the Christian faith but the ideology of the Führer. With great intensity the bishops led the battle for the preservation of parochial schools and for the upholding of the concordat, and the pastoral letters on this subject that our pastor read in church made a deep impression on me. Already then it dawned on me that, with their insistence on preserving institutions, these letters in part misread the reality. I mean that merely to guarantee institutions is useless if there are no people to support those institutions from inner conviction. But this was only partially the case. To be sure, teachers could be found in both the older and the younger generations who had deep convictions of faith, people who in their hearts saw Christian faith was the foundation of our culture and, therefore, of its work of education. But in the older generation there existed an anti-clerical resentment that was understandable, considering that the prerogative to inspect schools belonged to priests. In the younger generation there were convinced Nazis. So in both these cases it was inane to insist on an institutionally guaranteed Christianity. My teachers during the four years I went to school in Aschau were not exactly ardent Christians, and yet their attitude to the new movement was one of reserve. Because the Church was still the center of the village, not only in the sense of the physical building but also from the standpoint of the villagers' visceral outlook on life, it would not have been very smart to lash out violently against the Church. This would only have created opponents to the new regime.

There was, however, one very gifted young teacher who was quite enthusiastic about the new ideas. He attempted to make a breach in the solid structure of a village life that bore the deep imprint of the Church's liturgical year. So it was that he erected a Maypole with great pomp and circumstance and composed a kind of prayer to the Maypole as symbol of a life force perpetually renewing itself. The Maypole was supposed to bring back a portion of Germanic religion and thus help gradually to expel Christianity, which was now denounced as alienating Germans from their own great Germanic culture. He likewise organized midsummer sun festivals, again as a return to the sacredness of nature and to Germanic origins, to take the place of alien notions such as sin and redemption that had been imposed on us by foreign Jewish and Roman religion. When nowadays I hear how in many parts of the world Christianity is criticized as a destruction of individual cultural identity and an imposition of European values, I am amazed at how similar the types of argumentation are and at how familiar many a turn of phrase sounds. But in those days such rhetorical formulas hardly impressed the sober mentality of Bavarian farmers. The young men were more interested in the sausages that hung from the Maypole (which were grabbed by the fastest climbers) than in the high-flown phrases of the schoolteacher.

Another disquieting sign of the new times was the lighthouse that was erected on the Winterberg, one of the hills surrounding the village. At night, when it combed the sky with its glaring light, it appeared to us like a flash of lightning announcing a danger that still had no name. They said it was for sighting enemy airplanes. But in the skies over Aschau there were no airplanes at all, much less enemy ones. We vaguely perceived that what was here being prepared could only be reason for deep concern; but, in a world still apparently at total peace, no one could believe something sinister. As we were about to move away in 1937, we learned that construction of a "project" was being planned, which then almost immediately began to rise, carefully camouflaged, in the forest—an ammunitions factory that could not be seen from the air. What stood at the threshold began to take on frighteningly clear contours.

But, as I say, we did not ourselves see it. On the whole, village life continued as it always had. My brother became an altar boy ahead of me, and when he entered the *gymnasium* in Traunstein in 1935, and then the minor seminary of the archdiocese located in this town, I went in after him, although I could not compete with him in either zeal or diligence. Starting in the same year, my sister attended the middle school for girls in the nearby convent in Au am Inn. The school was run by Franciscan sisters in an old monastery of Augustinian canons that possessed one of the beautiful Baroque churches of our Bavarian homeland. For the time being the Church still remained an important force in the area of education, even if the school in Au already began to suffer certain vexations. The life of farmers was still organically structured in such a way that it enjoyed a firm symbiosis with the faith of the Church: birth and death, weddings and illnesses, sowing time and harvest time—everything was encompassed by the faith. Even if personal life and opinions by no means always corresponded to the faith of the Church, nevertheless no one could conceive of dying without the Church or of experiencing the great events of life without her. Life then would have simply fallen into the void, would have lost the solid ground that supported it and gave it meaning. People did not then go to Communion as frequently as today, but there were fixed occasions for the reception of the sacraments that hardly anyone would have thought of evading. A person who could not show the voucher affirming that he had made his Easter duty would have been regarded as antisocial. When people say nowadays that all of this was very external and superficial, I am only too glad to agree that many surely acted more out of social compulsion than interior conviction. And yet it was not altogether meaningless that during the Easter season even prominent farmers who were really owners of big estates had to make themselves small, kneel in the confessional, and accuse themselves of being sinners like the least of their farmhands and serving girls, of which there were still a great number in those days. Surely this moment of self-humbling, in which all differences in social status vanished, was not without effect.

The Church year gave the time its rhythm, and I experienced that with great gratitude and joy already as a child, indeed, above all as a child. During Advent the "liturgy of the angels" [Rorate Mass] was celebrated at dawn with great solemnity in the pitch-black church illuminated only with candles. The anticipated joy of Christmas gave the gloomy December days their own particular character. Every year our nativity scene grew by a few figures, and it was always a special joy to go gather moss, juniper, and pine branches with Father. During Lent, on Thursdays, "Mount of Olives" devotions were held, whose seriousness and sense of trust in God always penetrated deeply into my soul. Then, on Holy Saturday evening, the celebration of the Resurrection was especially impressive. Throughout Holy Week black curtains had covered the windows of the church so that even during the day the whole space was filled by a mysterious darkness. When the pastor sang the words "Christ is risen!" the curtains would suddenly fall, and the space would be flooded by radiant light. This was the most impressive portrayal of the Lord's Resurrection that I can conceive of. The liturgical movement that was then reaching its climax did not leave our village wholly unaffected. The pastor began to organize community Masses for the students in which a *Schott*, or missal, was used to read the texts of the Mass and pray the responses together.

What was this *Schott*? Toward the end of the nineteenth century the Benedictine monk Anselm Schott, of Beuron Abbey, translated the missal of the Church into German. Certain editions were in German only; others had a portion of the texts printed in Latin and German; and there were still others in which the complete Latin text appeared with the German text in parallel. A progressive pastor had given my parents their *Schott* as a gift on their wedding day in 1920, and so this was my family's prayerbook from the beginning. Our parents helped us from early on to understand the liturgy. There was a children's prayerbook adapted from the missal in which the unfolding of the sacred action was portrayed in pictures, so we could follow closely what was happening. Next to each picture there was a simple prayer that summarized the essentials of each part of the liturgy and adapted it to a child's mode of prayer. I was then given a *Schott* for children, in which the liturgy's basic texts themselves were printed. Then I got a *Schott* for Sundays, which contained the complete liturgy for Sundays and feast days. Finally, I received the complete missal for every day of the year. Every new step into the liturgy was a great event for me. Each new book I was given was something precious to me, and I could not dream of anything more beautiful. It was a riveting adventure to move by degrees into the mysterious world of the liturgy, which was being enacted before us and for us there on the altar. It was becoming more and more clear to me that here I was encountering a reality that no one had simply thought up, a reality that no official authority or great individual had created. This mysterious fabric of texts and actions had grown from the faith of the Church over the centuries. It bore the whole weight of history within itself, and yet, at the same time, it was much more than the product of human history. Every century had left its mark upon it. The introductory notes informed us about what came from the early Church, what from the Middle Ages, and what from modern times. Not everything was logical. Things sometimes got complicated, and it was not always easy to find one's way. But precisely this is what made the whole edifice wonderful, like one's own home. Naturally, the child I then was did not grasp every aspect of this, but I started down the road of the liturgy, and this became a continuous process of growth into a grand reality transcending all particular individuals and generations, a reality that became an occasion for me of ever-new amazement and discovery. The inexhaustible reality of the Catholic liturgy has accompanied me through all phases of life, and so I shall have to speak of it time and again.

3

Gymnasium Years in Traunstein

Because of the considerable physical demands that the profession made on them, policemen in those days were required to retire at age sixty. My father waited impatiently for this day. The frequent night shifts were beginning to get the better of him, but the greater stress came from the political situation within which he had to discharge his responsibilities. He took an extended sick leave, during which he and I would often go hiking and he would tell me stories of his earlier life. Finally, on March 6, 1937, he turned sixty. Back in 1933 my parents had bought an old, inexpensive farmhouse that stood at the edge of Traunstein. If I remember correctly, the year 1726 was etched into one of the beams holding up the ceiling. The former owners had cultivated the grounds, and so the house came with a big meadow where two enormous cherry trees as well as apple, pear, and plum trees grew. The property was bounded on one side by a grove of oak trees that you could reach by taking only a few steps, and on the other side of that you could wander for hours in an endless pine forest. The buildings were constructed in the Alpine style of the Salzburg region, with the hayloft and stalls under the same roof as the family quarters. The roof over the stalls and lofts was still covered with wooden shingles that were held down with stones against the wind. There was no running water but rather a well in front of the house that gave us wonderfully fresh water. Later, when other houses with wells began to be built all around, however, again and again our well would run dry in times of dry weather. The windows of the bedroom where we two boys slept faced south. When we opened the curtains in the morning we could almost reach out and touch Traunstein's two "local" mountains, the Hochfellen and the Hochgern. Over the years our mother created a splendid home from the slightly dilapidated house that Father had fixed up. From the windows hung flower boxes, and Mother planted two gardens in which all manner of useful things grew but which were always bordered with flowers in abundance. The structural condition of this house caused Father all kinds of trouble, but for us children it was a paradise beyond our wildest dreams. There were several roomy sheds full of mysteries and also a shadowy weaving room in which the former owners had practiced this skill. And then there were the meadow, the well, the trees, the forest . . . After all our wanderings this is where we finally found our true home, and it is here that my memory always returns with gratitude. I will never forget our first sight of the house. The truck with the furniture had gone on ahead of us, and we arrived in the car of our landlady in Aschau. What we first saw was the meadow, strewn with primroses. It was the beginning of April.

With our move to Traunstein, however, new and serious concerns entered my life. A few days after our arrival the school opened its doors. I now entered the first class in the "humanistic *gymnasium*", what today would be called the "*gymnasium* for classical languages". I had to walk about a half hour to get to school, which gave me ample time for looking about and reflecting, but also for reviewing what I had learned in school. Toward the end, the elementary school in Aschau had had little to offer, but now I found myself subject to a new discipline and new demands, especially since I was the youngest and one of the smallest in the whole class. Latin, as the foundation of one's whole education, was then still taught with old-fashioned rigor and thoroughness, something I have remained grateful for all my life. As a student of theology later on, I had no difficulty in studying the sources in Latin and Greek, and, at the time of the Council in Rome, although I had never attended lectures in Latin, I was quickly able to take part in the discussions conducted in the theological Latin then spoken.

In the meantime, National Socialism had not yet been able to change any more in the Traunstein *gymnasium* than it had in my school in Aschau. Not one of the professors of classical studies who belonged to the old guard had joined the Party, despite the considerable pressure exerted on government employees. Soon after I arrived at the *gymnasium*, the second headmaster was removed from his post because he did not bend to the new masters. In retrospect it seems to me that an education in Greek and Latin antiquity created a mental attitude that resisted seduction by a totalitarian ideology. Recently I thumbed through the songbook we then used, which already contained a number of Nazi songs, or old songs with Nazi words inserted, alongside valuable old songs. And I saw how our music teacher, a convinced Catholic, had had us cross out the phrase *"Juda den Tod"* [to Judah death] and write instead *"Wende die Not"* [dispel our plight]. But within a year of my arrival in the *gymnasium*, an emphatic "reform" began. Until then the humanistic *gymnasium* and the scientific school [*Realschule*] had existed side by side as two separate institutions. Now they became blended into a new type of school, the so-called *Oberschule,* in which the study of Greek completely disappeared, Latin was greatly diminished, with instruction beginning only in the third year, and in which modern languages, especially English, and the natural sciences instead received much greater weight. With the new type of school also came a new and younger generation of teachers, among whom one could certainly find many with excellent talents but also many who were now decided defenders of the new regime. Three years later religious instruction was banned from the schools, with its place taken by physical education and sports. But thank God that a concession was made: whoever had already begun under the old system of the humanistic *gymnasium* could conclude his studies by and large according to that model, the plan being of course that this form of education would die out on its own.

In the meantime, the rumbling of thunder in world history was also becoming more audible. Early in 1938 no one could ignore the movement of troops. There was talk of war against Austria, until one day we heard that the German army had marched into that country and that there had taken place the *Anschluss*, or "annexation" to the German Reich of Austria, which from now on would be known as "Greater Germany". For us, the seizure of power in Austria by the brown rulers clearly had a positive aspect. The borders of this neighboring country had been closed by Hitler. I still remember how one time we made an outing from Aschau to our beloved Tittmoning, but the bridge over the Salzach River, which we had so often traversed, was barred. It was no longer a bridge but a border. But now Austria was open again, although of course at a high price. From that day on we often went with our parents to nearby Salzburg, where we never failed to make the pilgrimage up to Maria Plain, visit the glorious churches, and breathe in the atmosphere of this unique city. Quite soon my brother took the initiative of getting acquainted with yet another dimension of Salzburg life. Because of the war, the international public could no longer come to the famous music festival, and so one could get rather good tickets at a very low price. So it was that we were able to go to performances of Beethoven's Ninth Symphony (conducted by Knappertsbusch), Mozart's Mass in C-minor, and a concert by the Regensburger Domspatzen [the "Cathedral Sparrows (boys' choir) of Regensburg"].

About this time a quite radical change occurred in my life. For two years I had been very happily going from home to school every day, but now the pastor urged me to enter the minor seminary in order to be initiated systematically into the spiritual life. For my father, whose pension was very scant indeed, this represented a great sacrifice. But my sister, after receiving her diploma from the scientific school and doing the obligatory year of service in agriculture, found a job in 1939 with a big company in Traunstein, and this eased the family budget. And so the decision was made, and at Easter of 1939, I entered the seminary. I did so with joy and great expectations because my brother had told me many exciting things about the place and because I developed good friendships with the seminarians in my class. However, I am one of those people who are not made for living in a boarding school. While at home I had lived and studied with great freedom, as I wished, and had built a childhood world of my own. Now I had to sit in a study hall with about sixty other boys, and this was such a torture to me that studying, which had always come so easily to me, now appeared almost impossible. But the greatest burden for me was the imposition of a progressive idea of education: every day for two hours we had to participate in sports in the big playground of the seminary. If this became such a complete torture for me, it was because, in the first place, I am not at all gifted at sports and also because I was the youngest of all the boys, some of whom were as much as three years older than I. Thus, I was inferior to most in physical strength. I must say that my fellow students were very tolerant of me, but in the long run it is not very pleasant to have to live on others' tolerance, knowing that you are nothing but a burden for the team to which you are assigned.

Meanwhile the drama of history was becoming increasingly grave with every violent act of the Third Reich. The crisis in the Sudetenland was ignited and fanned into full flame by a mechanism of lies that even someone half blind could see through. It was clear that the Munich Treaty of autumn 1938, which sanctioned the annexation of the Sudetenland by the Third Reich, was only a postponement of, not a solution to, the problem. My father could not understand how the French, of whom he had a very high opinion, could appear to accept one breach of law by Hitler after another as something quite normal. Early in 1939 Czechoslovakia was occupied, and on September 1 of the same year war broke out after a new campaign against Poland according to the same ritual. The war was still far from us, but the future stood there—sinister, threatening, impenetrable. The immediate result of the outbreak of war was that the minor seminary was declared a military hospital, so now, together with my brother, I again began to live at home and walk to school. But the director found alternate quarters for the seminary, first in the spa of the city (which, if our pastor, Father Kneipp, had had his way, would have become one big Kneipp city), and then in the English Sisters' institute for girls, located in Sparz, high over the city. Since the Nazis had closed all convent schools, their house stood mostly empty, and the community of seminarians could be lodged there. There was, however, no place for sports, so instead we took group hikes in the afternoons in the extensive woods of the surrounding area and played at the nearby mountain stream. We built dams, caught fish, and so forth. It was the kind of happy life boys should have. I came to terms, then, with being in the seminary and experienced a wonderful time in my life. I had to learn how to fit into the group, how to come out of my solitary ways and start building a community with others by giving and receiving. For this experience I am very grateful because it was important for my subsequent life.

At first the war appeared to be almost unreal. After Hitler had brutally brought down Poland in league with Stalin's Soviet Union, things became quiet. The Western powers seemed undecided, and on the front with France practically nothing was happening. Then came 1940, the year of Hitler's great triumphs: Denmark and Norway were occupied; Holland, Belgium, Luxembourg, and France were brought to their knees in a short time. Even people who were opposed to National Socialism experienced a kind of patriotic satisfaction. Hubert Jedin, the great historian of the Church councils and later on my colleague in Bonn (who, being half-Jewish, had had to flee Germany to spend the Hitler years in involuntary exile in Vatican City), has poignantly described in his memoirs the remarkable rift in his feelings occasioned by the events of this year. My father, however, was one who with unfailing clairvoyance saw that a victory of Hitler's would not be a victory for Germany but rather a victory of the Antichrist that would surely usher in apocalyptic times for all believers, and not only for them.

The war continued to go its inexorable way. The Balkans were next subjected to Hitler's domination. A cause for doubts and unease was the fact that the great invasion of Britain that had been announced was ever more delayed. I will never forget that sunny Sunday in 1941 when we received news that Germany had launched with her allies an attack against the Soviet Union on a front reaching from the North Pole to the Black Sea. On this day my class had arranged a little boat trip on a neighboring lake. The outing was fine, but the news about this new extension of the war hung over us like a nightmare and spoiled our joy. This could only take a turn for the worse. We thought of Napoleon; we thought of Russia's immeasurable distances where somewhere the German attack had to run aground.

The consequences were soon evident: huge transports now began to roll in, in some cases bringing home horribly wounded soldiers. Now every available space was turned into a military hospital. All suitable houses, including ours in Sparz, were confiscated. Seminarians who came from other towns and villages (practically all) had to look around for lodging with families. My brother and I now came home for good. It was also clear, moreover, that the war would last for a long time yet, and so it entered our life in earnest in an ever more threatening way. My brother was seventeen years old, and I, fourteen. Perhaps I would be spared. But we could foresee that there would be no escape for my brother. In the summer of 1942, he was in fact taken into the so-called *Reichsarbeitsdienst* [work service of the Reich], and then in the fall he was drafted into the army, where he was assigned to the signal corps as a radio operator. After tours of duty in France, Holland, and Czechoslovakia, he was sent to the Italian front in 1944, where he was wounded. And so, strangely enough, he returned to the seminary in Traunstein, for him the place where he had spent so many wonderful years, but now converted into a military hospital. Immediately after his convalescence, however, he had to return to the front in Italy.

Despite the grimness of the historical situation, I was facing a good year at home and at the *gymnasium* in Traunstein. The Greek and Latin classics filled me with enthusiasm, and mathematics, too, had in the meantime caught my interest. Above all, I now discovered literature. I assiduously studied the history of literature, read Goethe with delight, was a bit put off by Schiller's moralism, and particularly loved nineteenth-century writers like Eichendorff, Mörike, and Stifter, while others like Raabe and Kleist remained somewhat alien. Naturally I myself began to write with great zeal and returned with renewed joy to the liturgical texts, which I now tried to translate from the original in an improved and more vital way. This was a time of interior exaltation, full of hope for the great things that were gradually opening up to me in the boundless realm of the spirit. Alongside this experience, however, there also stood the fact that almost every day the newspaper informed us of some soldier's death, and almost every day a requiem Mass had to be held for a young man. The names brushed us more and more closely. Increasingly we recognized the names of *gymnasium* schoolmates who only a short while before had been our classmates, full of confidence and the joy of life.

4

War Service and Imprisonment

Because of the increasingly worn-down condition of the men in the armed forces, our rulers came up with something new in 1943. They observed that boarding-school students already had to live in community away from their homes and that, therefore, nothing stood in the way of changing the place where they boarded—namely, to the batteries of the anti-aircraft defense (Flak). And since in any event they could not be studying the whole day, it appeared quite normal to engage them in their free time for the service of defense against enemy planes. Even though I had not for quite a while now been in boarding school, still, juridically, I belonged to the minor seminary in Traunstein. So it was that the small group of seminarians from my class (those born in 1926 and 1927) were now drafted, and we had to go to the Flak in Munich. Being all of sixteen years of age, I now had to undertake a very peculiar kind of "boarding-school" existence. We lived in barracks like the regular soldiers, who were of course in the minority, wore uniforms similar to theirs, and basically had to perform the same services as they, with the only difference being that on the side we had in addition a reduced load of courses, given by the teachers of the renowned Maximilians-Gymnasium in Munich. In many respects this was an interesting experience. We now formed one class with the actual students of this *gymnasium*, who had likewise been drafted into the Flak, and so we entered a world that was new to us. Those of us from Traunstein were better in Latin and Greek, but we became aware that we had lived in the provinces and that the big city, with its multitude of cultural offerings, had opened other horizons to our new schoolmates. At first there was a lot of friction, but with time we all grew together to form a good community.

Our first location was Ludwigsfeld, to the north of Munich, where we had to protect a branch of the Bavarian Motor Works (BMW) that produced motors for airplanes. Then we went to Unterföhring, to the northwest of Munich, and for a brief time to Innsbruck, where the railroad station had been destroyed and protection seemed necessary. When no more attacks took place there, we were finally transferred to Gilching, just north of Lake Ammer, with a double commission: we had to defend the nearby Dornier-Werke, from which the first jets soared into the air, and, more generally, we had to stop the Allied flyers who gathered in this area for attacks on Munich.

I need not belabor the fact that my time with the Flak brought many an unpleasantness, particularly for so nonmilitary a person as myself. And yet I remember Gilching very fondly. There I belonged to telephone communications, and the noncommissioned officer in charge of us defended the autonomy of our group with tooth and nail. We were exempt from all military exercises, and no one dared to intrude into our little world. Autonomy reached its high point when I was assigned living quarters in the neighboring battery and, for inscrutable reasons, even got a room all to myself—primitive, but a real single room. Outside my hours of service, I could now do whatever I wanted and cultivate my interests without any hindrance. Besides, there was a

surprisingly large group of active Catholics here who organized religious instruction and occasionally led visits to
churches. And so, paradoxically, this summer is inscribed in
my memory as a wonderful time of largely independent
living.

To be sure, the overall climate of contemporary history
was anything but encouraging. Early in the year our battery
had been directly attacked, with one dead and many
wounded as a result. In the summer, systematic large-scale
attacks on Munich began. Three times a week we were still
allowed to travel into the city to attend classes at the Max-
Gymnasium; but every time it was frightening to see new
destruction and to experience how the city was falling into
ruins bit by bit. The air was more and more filled with
smoke and the smell of fire. In the end, regular train service
was no longer possible. In this situation, most of us came to
look on the Western allies' invasion of France, which finally
began in July, as a sign of hope. Basically there was great trust
in the Western powers and a hope that their sense of justice
would also help Germany to begin a new and peaceful existence. However, which of us would live to experience it?
None of us could be sure that he would live to return home
from this inferno.

On September 10, 1944, having reached military age, we
were released from the Flak, in which we had actually served
as students. When I arrived home, the draft notice of the
Reichsarbeitsdienst already lay on the table. On September 20
an endless trip took us to Burgenland, where we (including
many friends from the *gymnasium* at Traunstein) were assigned to a camp in a spot where three countries—Austria,
Czechoslovakia, and Hungary—meet. The weeks spent in
the labor detail have left me with oppressive memories. Most
of our superiors were former members of the so-called Aus-

trian Legion and thus old Nazis who had done time in prison under Chancellor Dollfuß. They were fanatical ideologues who tyrannized us without respite. One night we were pulled out of bed and gathered together, half asleep in our exercise uniforms. An SS officer had each individual come forward and, by taking advantage of our exhaustion and exposing each of us before the gathered group, attempted to make "voluntary" recruits for the weapons branch of the SS. A whole series of good-natured friends were in this way forced into this criminal group. With a few others I had the good fortune of being able to say that I intended to become a Catholic priest. We were sent out with mockery and verbal abuse. But these insults tasted wonderful because they freed us from the threat of that deceitful "voluntary service" and all its consequences.

To begin with, we were trained according to a ritual invented in the 1930s, which was adapted from a kind of "cult of the spade", that is, a cult of work as redemptive power. An intricate military drill taught us how to lay down the spade solemnly, how to pick it up and swing it over the shoulder. The cleaning of the spade, which was not to show a single speck of dust, was among the essential elements of this pseudo-liturgy. This world of appearances suddenly collapsed overnight when neighboring Hungary, at whose border we were stationed, surrendered in October to the Russians, who in the meantime had penetrated deep into the center of the country. We thought we could hear the din of artillery at a distance; the front was drawing closer. Now the rituals with the spade came to an end, and every day we had to ride out to erect a so-called southwestern rampart: tank blockades and trenches, which we, along with an enormous army of allegedly volunteer workers from every country in Europe, had to dig directly across the fertile clay soil of

Burgenland's vineyards. When we went home exhausted in the evening, the spades, which previously could not have a single speck of dust, now hung from the wall full of big clods of clay; but no one cared. Precisely this fall of the spade from cultic object to banal tool for everyday use allowed us to perceive the deeper collapse taking place there. A full-scale liturgy and the world behind it were being unmasked as a lie.

It was common practice, as the front drew closer, for those engaged in the work detail simply to be taken into the military. This is what we expected. But, to our grateful astonishment, something different happened. In the end, all work on the southwest rampart was stopped, and we lived in our camp without further orders. No cries of command were now heard, and an eerie, hollow silence reigned. On November 20 our suitcases with our civilian clothes were given back to us, and we were loaded onto railway cars. We thus undertook a journey home that was continually interrupted by air-raid alarms. Vienna, which only in September had still remained untouched by the events of the war, now showed the scars of bombs. I was even more strongly affected by the fact that in my beloved Salzburg not only did the train station lie in ruins, but it was evident from far off that the city's splendid centerpiece—the huge Renaissance cathedral—had been heavily damaged. If I remember correctly, the dome had caved in. Since, because of danger from the air, the train had to pass through Traunstein without stopping, the only thing to do was to jump off. It was an idyllically beautiful fall day. There was a bit of hoarfrost on the trees, and the mountains glowed in the afternoon sun. Seldom have I ever experienced the beauty of my homeland as on this return from a world disfigured by ideology and hatred.

Much to my amazement there was still no notice on the table drafting me into military service, as I might have ex-

pected. I had been granted almost three weeks for both
interior and exterior renewal. Then we were called to
Munich, where we were informed of our different destina-
tions. The officer in charge was quite openly critical of the
war and Hitler's system. He showed much understanding for
us and tried to find the best possible assignment for each of
us, the thing that would be most bearable. Thus, he assigned
me to the infantry barracks in Traunstein, and with fatherly
kindness he encouraged me to take a few more free days at
home without rushing to report to my new post. The atmosphere I found in the barracks was a pleasant change from
what I had known in the labor service. It is true that the head
of the company liked to shout and that he apparently was still
a faithful devotee of Nazism. But those in charge of our
formation were experienced men who had tasted the horrors
of war at the front and who did not want to make things
more difficult for us than they already were. We celebrated
Christmas in our living quarters with a heavy mood. Serving
in the same unit with us young men there were several heads
of families, nearly forty years of age, who, despite health
problems, had now been called to arms in the last year of the
war. My heart was deeply moved by their homesickness for
wives and children. It was already difficult enough for them
to be subjected to military drills like schoolboys along with
us, who were twenty years their junior. After basic training,
beginning in mid-January, we were continually relocated to
different posts all around Traunstein, but, on account of
an illness, I was largely exempt from military duty. Very
strangely, we were not called to the front, which was drawing ever nearer. But we were given new uniforms and had to
march through Traunstein singing war songs, perhaps in order to show the civilian population that the Führer still had
young and freshly trained soldiers at his disposal. Hitler's

death finally strengthened our hope that things would soon end. The unhurried manner of the American advance, however, deferred more and more the day of liberation.

At the end of April or the beginning of May—I do not remember precisely—I decided to go home. I knew that the city was surrounded by soldiers who had orders to shoot deserters on the spot. For this reason I used a little-known back road out of town, hoping to get through unmolested. But, as I walked out of a railroad underpass, two soldiers were standing at their posts, and for a moment the situation was extremely critical for me. Thank God that they, too, had had their fill of war and did not want to become murderers. Still, they had to find an excuse to let me go. Because of an injury I had my arm in a sling, and so they said: "Comrade, you are wounded. Move on!" In this way I came home unhurt. Sitting at the table were some of the English Sisters whom my sister knew well. They were poring over a map and trying to determine when we could finally count on the Americans' arrival. When I walked in, they thought that the presence of a soldier would be a sure protection for the house, but of course the opposite was the case. In the course of the next few days there lodged with us, first, a sergeant-major of the air force, an agreeable Catholic from Berlin, who, following a strange logic we could not understand, still believed in the victory of the "German Reich". My father, who argued extensively with him on this matter, was finally able to win him over to the other side. Then two SS men were given shelter in our house, which made the situation doubly dangerous. They could not fail to see that I was of military age, and so they began to make inquiries about my status. It was a known fact that a number of soldiers who had left their units had already been hanged from trees by SS men. Besides, my father could not help voicing all his ire against Hitler to their faces, which as a rule should have had deadly consequences for him. But a special angel seemed to be guarding us, and the two disappeared the next day without having caused any mischief.

The Americans finally arrived in our village. Even though our house lacked all comfort, they chose it as their headquarters. I was identified as a soldier, had to put back on the uniform I had already abandoned, had to raise my hands and join the steadily growing throng of war prisoners whom they were lining up on our meadow. It especially cut my good mother's heart to the quick to see her boy and the rest of the defeated army standing there, exposed to an uncertain fate, prisoners under the custody of heavily armed Americans. We had hopes of being released soon, but Father and Mother quickly put together a number of things that could be useful for the road ahead, and I myself slipped a big empty notebook and a pencil into my pocket—which seemed a most impractical choice, but this notebook became a wonderful companion to me, because day by day I could enter into it thoughts and reflections of all kinds. I even tried my hand at Greek hexameters. During three days of marching, we advanced on the empty expressway in a column moving toward Bad Aibling that was gradually becoming endless. The American soldiers liked especially to take pictures of us, the youngest ones, and also of the oldest, in order to take home with them souvenirs of the defeated army and the woeful condition of its personnel. Then for a few days we lay about in an open field at the military airport of Bad Aibling, until we were shipped off to an area of enormous farmlands near Ulm, where about fifty thousand prisoners had been brought. The magnitude of these numbers apparently taxed the abilities of the Americans themselves. Until the end of our captivity, we slept outdoors. Our rations consisted of one ladleful of soup and a little bread per day. A few fortunate individuals had brought a tent with them into the prisoner-of-war camp. When, after a period of good weather, the rains started, "tent clubs" began to be formed for primitive protection against the inclemency of the weather. In front of us, at the very horizon, rose the majestic contours of the Ulm cathedral. Day after day the sight of it was for me like a consoling proclamation of the indestructible humaneness of faith. In the camp itself, moreover, numerous initiatives were undertaken to lend help. There were a few priests present who now celebrated Holy Mass every day in the open air. Those who came were not exactly a huge crowd, but they were grateful indeed. Theological students in their final semesters, and also academicians of different backgrounds (jurists, art historians, philosophers), began to meet formally, so that a wide-ranging program of conferences developed that brought some structure to our empty days. Real knowledge was imparted, and slowly friendships began to grow across the different blocks of the camp. We lived without a clock, without a calendar, without newspapers; only through rumors—often strangely distorted and confused—did something of what was happening in the larger world penetrate through the barbed-wire fence into our own separate world. Then, around the beginning of June, if I remember correctly, the releases began, and every new gap in our ranks was a sign of hope. The different occupations determined the order of release: farmers first, and last of all—because the least needed in this situation—students. Quite a few academicians understandably declared themselves to be farmers, and very many suddenly remembered a distant relative or acquaintance in Bavaria in order to be released into that region, because the American sector appeared to be the most secure and promising. Finally it was my turn, too. On June 19, 1945, I had to pass through the various inspections and interrogations, until, overjoyed, I held in my hand the certificate of release that made the end of the war a reality for me, too. We were brought by American trucks to the northern edge of Munich, and then each of us had to fend for himself in finding a way to get home. I teamed up with a young man from Trostberg, in the vicinity of Traunstein, to find our way home together. In three days we hoped to cover the 120 or so kilometers that separated us from our families. We planned to spend the night along the way with farming families, who would also give us a bite to eat. We had passed Ottobrunn when we were overtaken by a truck, powered by wood gas and loaded with milk. Both of us were too shy to signal to it, but the driver stopped on his own and asked us where we were headed. He laughed when we said that Traunstein was our destination, because he worked for a dairy in Traunstein and was now on his way home. So it was that, unexpectedly, I arrived in my home city even before sunset; the heavenly Jerusalem itself could not have appeared more beautiful to me at that moment. I heard praying and singing coming from the church: it was the evening of the Feast of the Sacred Heart of Jesus. I did not want to create a disturbance, so I did not go in. Rather, I rushed home as fast as I could. My father could hardly believe it as I suddenly stood there before him, alive and well. My mother and sister were in church. On the way home they learned from some girls that they had seen me rushing by. In my whole life I have never again had so magnificent a meal as the simple one that Mother then prepared for me from the vegetables of her own garden.

Yet something was still missing to make our joy complete. Since the beginning of April there had been no news from my brother. And so a quiet sorrow hung over our house. What an explosion of delight, then, when one hot July day we suddenly heard steps, and the one we had missed for so long suddenly stood there in our midst, with a brown tan from the Italian sun. Full of thanksgiving at his deliverance, he now sat down at the piano and intoned the hymn "Grosser Gott, wir loben dich" [Holy God, we praise thy Name]. The months that followed were full of a sense of newly won freedom, something we were only now learning really to treasure, and this period belongs to the most beautiful memories of my entire life. Little by little all of us who had been strewn so far apart began to gather again. We were continually searching each other out, exchanging recollections and comparing plans for our new life. My brother and I worked with other returnees to make the seminary buildings—so run down after six years as a military hospital—again usable for their intended purpose. No books could be bought in a Germany that lay desolate and in a total economic shambles. But we could borrow some from the pastor and the seminary and so attempt to take our first steps into the unknown land of philosophy and theology. My brother devoted himself passionately to music, his particular gift. At Christmas we were able to organize a class reunion. Many had fallen in the war, and we who had returned home were all the more grateful for the gift of life and for the hope that again rose high above all destruction.

5

In the Seminary at Freising

The major seminary at Freising, our destination, was for the moment serving as a military hospital for foreign prisoners of war, who were being treated with a view to their repatriation. And so the seminary could not open its doors as quickly as had been hoped. One first small group of advanced students was able to move into a few vacated rooms in November 1945. By Christmas the rest of the candidates had already moved into temporary accommodations, although a large portion of the house was still being used for the other purpose. This was a very mixed group indeed, the 120 or so seminarians who now came together in Freising to set out on the road to the priesthood. The span of ages ranged from some who were nearly forty down to a few of us who were nineteen. Many had been enlisted for the whole length of the war, and almost all had been soldiers for some years: they had gone through trials and terrors that would leave a deep mark on their lives. It was understandable that many of the older combatants looked down on us youngsters as immature children who lacked the sufferings necessary for the priestly ministry, since we had not gone through those dark nights that alone can give full shape to the radical assent a priest must give. Despite the extreme differences of our experiences and perspectives, we were all bound together by a great sense of gratitude for having been allowed to return home from the abyss of those difficult years. This gratitude now created a common will to make up finally for everything we had neglected and to serve Christ in his Church for new and better times, for a better Germany, and for a better world. No one doubted that the Church was the locus of all our hopes. Despite many human failings, the Church was the alternative to the destructive ideology of the brown rulers; in the inferno that had swallowed up the powerful, she had stood firm with a force coming to her from eternity. It had been demonstrated: The gates of hell will not overpower her. From our own experience we now knew what was meant by "the gates of hell", and we could also see with our own eyes that the house built on rock had stood firm.

Gratitude and a will to make a new start, to be active in the Church and for the sake of the world: these were the feelings that characterized the seminary community. Together with this came a hunger for knowledge that had grown in the years of famine, in the years when we had been delivered up to the Moloch of power, so far from the realm of the spirit. Books were, I repeat, a rarity in a Germany that was destroyed and cut off from the rest of the world. Nevertheless, despite the bomb damage that had taken place here too, a rather good reference library had been preserved that could, so to speak, take the edge off our hunger. Our interests were varied. We wanted not only to do theology in the narrower sense but to listen to the voices of man today. We devoured the novels of Gertrud von Le Fort, Elisabeth Langgässer, and Ernst Wiechert. Dostoevsky was one of the authors everyone read, and likewise the great Frenchmen: Claudel, Bernanos, Mauriac. We also followed closely the recent developments in the natural sciences. We thought that, with the breakthroughs made by Planck, Heisenberg, and Einstein, the sciences were once again on their way to

God. The anti-religious orientation that had reached its climax with Haeckel had now been broken, and this gave us new hope. Aloys Wenzel, a philosopher from Munich who had first specialized in physics, wrote a much-read work, his *Philosophy of Freedom,* in which he tried to show that the determinist world view of classical physics, which left no room for God, had been dispelled by an open conception of the world in which there was room for something new, something unforeseen and incalculable. In the domain of theology and philosophy, the voices that moved us most directly were those of Romano Guardini, Josef Pieper, Theodor Häcker, and Peter Wust.

An important event for us was the fact that the prefect assigned to our study hall (there were no individual rooms) was a theologian only just returned from an English war prison. His name was Alfred Läpple, who later was to teach religious pedagogy in Salzburg and become one of the most renowned and prolific religious writers of our time. Already before the war he had begun work on a theological dissertation on the concept of conscience in Cardinal Newman, under the direction of Theodor Steinbüchel, a moral theologian in Munich. With his far-ranging knowledge of the history of philosophy and his taste for argumentation, Läpple became a great stimulus for us. I read Steinbüchel's two volumes on the philosophical foundations of moral theology, which had just appeared in a new edition, and in them I found a first-rate introduction to the thought of Heidegger and Jaspers as well as to the philosophies of Nietzsche, Klages, and Bergson. Almost more important for me was Steinbüchel's book *Der Umbruch des Denkens* [The revolution of thought]: here I read how, just as now we could affirm that physics was abandoning the mechanistic world view and turning toward a new openness to the unknown—and hence also to the known Unknown, namely, God—so, too, in philosophy we could detect a return to metaphysics, which had become inaccessible since Kant. After beginning his career with studies on Hegel and socialism, Steinbüchel was now portraying in this book (under the influence above all of Ferdinand Ebner) his discovery of personalism, which had become a major turning point in his own intellectual development. We then found the philosophy of personalism reiterated with renewed conviction in the great Jewish thinker Martin Buber. This encounter with personalism was for me a spiritual experience that left an essential mark, especially since I spontaneously associated such personalism with the thought of Saint Augustine, who in his *Confessions* had struck me with the power of all his human passion and depth. By contrast, I had difficulties in penetrating the thought of Thomas Aquinas, whose crystal-clear logic seemed to me to be too closed in on itself, too impersonal and ready-made. This may also have had something to do with the fact that Arnold Wilmsen, the philosopher who taught us Thomas, presented us with a rigid, neoscholastic Thomism that was simply too far afield from my own questions. And yet, in and of himself, Wilmsen was an interesting man. He had been a worker in the Ruhr region. The thirst for knowledge had made him save his money in order to study philosophy. His teachers in Munich had impressed him with the phenomenology rooted in Husserl, but that had not satisfied him. And so he went to Rome, and in the Thomistic philosophy taught there he found what he had been looking for. His enthusiasm and deep convictions were impressive, but now it seemed that he himself no longer asked questions but limited himself to defending passionately, against all questions, what he had found. But we, being young, were questioners above all. More helpful, on the other hand, was a four-semester course of lectures on the history of philosophy by a young professor, Jakob Fellermeier, who provided us with a comprehensive overview of the intellectual struggle, beginning with Socrates and the pre-Socratics up until the present. This gave me a foundation in philosophy for which I am still grateful today.

Our studies, as I have said, were propelled by our common hunger for knowledge. But they also had their proper human environment in the close community atmosphere that reigned in the seminary despite many differences in age and intellectual background. Largely responsible for this was our rector at the time, Michael Höck, who had been in the concentration camp at Dachau for five years and who soon acquired the nickname "the father" for his kindly and affectionate ways. We also played a lot of music in the house, and on festive occasions we had theatrical performances. But my most precious memories remain the great liturgical celebrations in the cathedral and the hours of silent prayer in the house chapel. The grand and venerable figure of Cardinal Faulhaber impressed me deeply. You could practically touch the burden of sufferings he had had to bear during the Nazi period, which now enveloped him with an aura of dignity. In him we were not just looking for "an accessible bishop"; rather, what moved me deeply about him was the awe-inspiring grandeur of his mission, with which he had become fully identified.

6

Theological Studies in Munich

Our two-year study of philosophy, prescribed by the curriculum of that time, came to an end in the summer semester of 1947, and now a decision had to be made. In order to explain it, I will have to go a little farther back. In Bavaria there were at that time two theological faculties located within state universities, one in Munich and the other in Würzburg. In Eichstätt there was a "Tridentine" seminary in the strict sense of the word, that is, a seminary for the formation of future priests with a faculty of its own answerable only to the bishop and responsible for the students' theological education. Each of five dioceses—among them Munich-Freising—had an episcopal seminary associated with a state theological faculty. In our diocese the seminary and the theological faculty were located in Freising. The Munich theological faculty, therefore, did not serve the priestly formation of only one diocese. This is why in Munich there was no diocesan seminary but rather the so-called Herzogliches Georgianum, which had been founded in 1494 in Ingolstadt by Duke George the Rich for candidates to the priesthood from the whole of Bavaria. This institution moved, along with the University of Ingolstadt, first to Landshut and then to Munich. After the erection of diocesan seminaries, its mission became to receive theological students who wanted to study at the university and had received their bishops' permission to this effect. With two other fellow students of my age, I decided to ask the bishop to allow me to study in Munich, and this is what occurred. My hope was to become more fully familiar with the intellectual debates of our time by working at the university, so as some day to be able to dedicate myself completely to theology as a profession.

The lack of fuel for heating made it impossible to have a regular winter semester; and so the academic year 1947–1948 began already on September 1. As compensation, we had some three and a half months of vacation from Christmas to Easter. We came together in Munich at the end of August to take part in the spiritual exercises that preceded the academic year. The university largely lay in ruins. For the most part the library was still inaccessible. The theological faculty had found temporary quarters in the former royal hunting lodge at Fürstenried, just south of Munich. This is where the unfortunate King Otto had spent the decades of his mental illness well into the First World War. After the end of the monarchy, the archdiocese had acquired the small castle and set up a retreat house within it. During the hard-pressed period of the 1920s, two modest annexes had been built in which a seminary for late vocations was established. It was in these two buildings that both the theological faculty and the Georgianum were now housed. The quarters were tight and crowded: one and the same building housed the living quarters for two professors; the theological faculty's administrative office as well as its meeting-room; then the libraries for pastoral theology, Church history, and both Old and New Testament exegesis; and in addition the students' study rooms and dormitory. Such narrow confines made bunk beds necessary. When I opened my eyes on the first morning, half asleep as I still was, I thought for a moment that we were back in the war again and that I had been transported to our Flak battery. Our diet, too, was sparse since we could not depend on our own farm as we had in Freising. The castle itself housed both a small military hospital for wounded foreign soldiers and the retreat center. The wonderful thing was that we could use the castle's beautiful park, which was divided into one area laid out in the French style and another with a garden in the English style. I wandered through this park over and over again, immersed in all sorts of thoughts. This is where the decisions of those years took shape, and also where I tried to think through and appropriate all of the knowledge imparted to us during the lectures. The atmosphere in the house was more reserved than in Freising. We did not have the spontaneous camaraderie I had known there. The extreme mixture of types was too great for this. Here there were students from all over Germany, particularly from the north of the country, and also doctoral candidates who were already quite advanced in their work. Intellectual concerns were dominant here, while in Freising the common will to be laboring soon in the care of souls united us in a much more direct way. Primary stress was put on the lectures, and these are what shaped the area of common interests and the exchange of questions and answers.

I looked forward with burning expectation to the lectures of our renowned teachers. To be sure, the setting was peculiar indeed. Since we had no lecture hall at our disposal, classes had to be held in the greenhouse of the castle garden. Here, we at first baked in glowing heat that could be rivaled only by the freezing cold of the winter. But at that time such externals hardly bothered us at all. I must interject here that the Munich theological faculty had been abolished by the Nazis in 1938 because Cardinal Faulhaber refused to give his approval to a professor who was known to be a Hitler sympathizer and whom the authorities wanted to install in the chair for canon law. In view of such interference outside the academic purview, the Nazi ministry of education declared, academic freedom could no longer be guaranteed; under such circumstances, therefore, the theological faculty could no longer continue to operate in Munich. This is the reason why, after the war, the faculty had to be wholly reconstituted from the ground up. A first move was to draw on the teaching bodies of two faculties—Breslau (in Silesia) and Braunsberg (in East Prussia)—that had ceased to exist because of the Polish occupation of territories east of the border formed by the Oder and Neiße Rivers and the resulting expulsion of Germans from that area. From Breslau came the professors for Old and New Testament (Stummer and Maier) as well as for Church history (Seppelt); and from Braunsberg the moral theologian Egenter (a priest from Passau) and the fundamental theologian Gottlieb Söhngen, who, being a native of Cologne, was a wonderful embodiment of the Rhenish temperament. From Münster came Michael Schmaus, a priest of the archdiocese of Munich, who had become renowned throughout Germany on account of his novel textbook of dogmatic theology. He had parted ways with neoscholastic schemas and composed a living presentation of the Catholic doctrine of the faith in the spirit of the liturgical movement and the recent return to Scripture and the Fathers, which had developed in the years after the First World War. And Schmaus brought two other important scholars with him from Münster: Josef Pascher, a pastoral theologian who had taught for a short time in the Munich faculty before the war, and Klaus Mörsdorf, a young professor of canon law who approached his subject very decidedly as a theological discipline and not as something peripheral to theology. He conceived of canon law as belonging at the very center of theology by virtue of the Incarnation, that is, as a logical consequence of the Word becoming man: the Word, thus, had associated himself with the necessity of institutional and legal forms. Pascher had made an interesting intellectual pilgrimage. He had first studied mathematics and learned Oriental languages; then he had worked in pedagogy and comparative religion and researched the mysticism of Philo of Alexandria; finally, by way of pastoral theology, he had arrived at the systematic study of the liturgy, which in the Munich years became his specialized field of work. As director of the Georgianum, he was responsible for our personal and priestly formation. This task he discharged inspired by the spirit of the liturgy, and his impact on our spiritual development was profound and decisive. Precisely the three different origins of our academic teachers gave the faculty great intellectual breadth and an interior richness that attracted students from all parts of Germany.

At that time the star of our faculty was beyond a doubt Friedrich Wilhelm Maier, professor for New Testament exegesis. He, too, had had an unusual life. As a young man he had received his *habilitation* (the degree qualifying one to teach at a German university) at the University of Strasbourg, which at that time belonged to the German Reich (and where coincidentally, in the period before 1911, Michael Faulhaber had been professor of Old Testament). As a brilliant young scholar, Maier had undertaken the interpretation of the synoptic Gospels for a biblical commentary then in the process of being written. In this commentary he proposed with vigor a theory that today is accepted by almost everyone, the so-called "two-source theory", according to which Mark and a collection of sayings of Jesus no longer extant (the "Q" source, from *Quelle*) are the basis for the

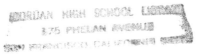
three synoptic Gospels. Mark, in other words, is accordingly the source for the later Gospels according to Matthew and Luke. This contradicts an ancient tradition, traceable all the way to the second century, which sees in Matthew the oldest Gospel, said to have been written by the apostle "in a Hebraic dialect". So it was that Maier walked right into the Modernist dispute, which at that time was being waged with great vehemence and whose focal point was precisely the question concerning the Gospels. The French scholar Loisy had practically rejected out of hand the credibility of the Gospels. The theories of liberal exegesis necessarily posed a threat to the very foundations of faith itself—a problem that is far from having been resolved today. Maier's thesis was perceived to be a surrender to liberalism, and so he had to leave the world of academic teaching. More than once he referred to the decree of "Recedat a cathedra" (Let him leave his chair) that was handed down by Rome. Thus, he first became a military chaplain, a task he exercised through the First World War. Afterward he became chaplain in a prison, whose inmates left him with very positive memories. In the changed climate of the 1920s, he could finally return to the academic world. In 1924 he was called to Breslau to teach New Testament, and both there and afterward in Munich he quickly won the hearts of his listeners. He never quite got over the trauma of having been dismissed. He harbored a certain bitterness against Rome, and this extended also to the archbishop of Munich, who, in Maier's view, behaved none too collegially toward him. These reservations aside, Maier was a man of deep faith and a priest who took great pains in the priestly formation of the young men entrusted to him.

His lectures were the only ones for which the greenhouse was too small; you had to arrive early to get a seat. But in many respects Maier belonged to a world that had already disappeared. He still cultivated the rhetoric of the turn of the century, which, at the beginning, I found impressive but, as time went on, a bit artificial and overdone. His exegetical approach, too, had remained that of the liberal age. With admirable diligence, it is true, he had read everything that had appeared in the meantime and also worked it into his lectures; but, in the end, the new epoch that Bultmann and Barth had ushered in, each in his own way, was really lost on him. In retrospect I would like to say that Maier offered a prime example of that orientation which Romano Guardini experienced in his teachers at Tübingen and which he characterized as "a liberalism restricted by dogma". Surely this is an insufficient position when compared with the new orientation that Guardini himself was perhaps the first to work out right in the midst of the Modernist drama, for Maier represents those who look upon dogma, not as a shaping force, but only as a shackle, a negation, and a limit in the construction of theology. And yet, from a distance of nearly fifty years, I can once again truly see what was positive there: the candid questions from the perspectives of the liberal-historical method created a new directness in the approach to Sacred Scripture and opened up dimensions of the text that were no longer perceived by the all-too-predetermined dogmatic reading. The Bible spoke to us with new immediacy and freshness. But those things in the liberal method that were arbitrary and tended to flatten out the Bible (just think of Harnack and his school) could be compensated for by obedience to dogma. A characteristic fruitfulness came from the balance between liberalism and dogma. So it was that, for the six semesters of my theological studies, I listened to and assimilated all of Maier's lectures with the greatest attention. Exegesis has always remained for me the center of my theological work. Maier is to be thanked for the fact that, for us, Sacred Scripture was "the soul of our theological studies", as the Second Vatican Council would later require. Even if I gradually became more aware of the weaknesses in Maier's approach—it is not in a position to see the full depth of the figure of Christ—still, everything I heard from him and learned by way of method remains fundamental to me.

In contrast to the striking quality of Maier's figure, the professor for Old Testament, Friedrich Stummer, was a quiet and reserved man whose strength was strictly historical and philological work; he would hint at theological themes only with the greatest restraint. But I greatly appreciated this scholarly carefulness, and, besides being an eager listener at his lectures, I also participated in his seminars. Thus it was that the Old Testament was opened up and became precious for me. More and more I came to understand why the New Testament is not a different book of a different religion that, for some reason or other, had appropriated the Holy Scriptures of the Jews as a kind of preliminary structure. The New Testament is nothing other than an interpretation of "the Law, the Prophets, and the Writings" found from or contained in the story of Jesus. Now, this "Law, Prophets, and Writings" had not yet, at the time of Jesus, grown together to form a definitive canon; rather, they were still openended and, as such, offered themselves spontaneously to Jesus' disciples as a testimony to him, as the Sacred Scriptures that revealed his mystery. I have ever more come to the realization that Judaism (which, strictly speaking, begins with the end of the formation of the canon, that is, in the first century after Christ) and the Christian faith described in the New Testament are two ways of appropriating Israel's Scriptures, two ways that, in the end, are both determined by the position one assumes with regard to the figure of Jesus of

Nazareth. The Scripture we today call Old Testament is in itself open to both ways. For the most part, only after the Second World War did we begin to understand that the Jewish interpretation, too, in the time "after Christ", of course possesses a theological mission of its own.

But let us return to 1947. Even we novices in theology could soon tell that the Breslau group was not different from the professors coming from Münster and Braunsberg only with respect to age. (All the scholars from Breslau were over sixty.) They also embodied a different era in theology. The two exegetes and (with a lower profile) the Church historian embodied the liberal era, in the best sense of the term. Particularly the three professors from Münster, on the other hand, but also the two from Braunsberg, had been molded by the theological change that took place along with the more general change in outlook after the First World War. With its million dead, with all the horrors that technology made possible as an instrument of war, the First World War was experienced as the collapse of the liberal dogma of progress and, hence, of the liberal world view as such. It was precisely with the help of modern achievements that the destruction of man and his dignity was achieved that had not been possible before. Under the shock of this experience, people now turned again to what previously had been looked upon as superseded: namely, the Church, the liturgy, the sacraments, and this not only in the Catholic sphere but especially in the Protestant world. Karl Barth's *Epistle to the Romans* became a declaration of war on liberalism and a manifesto of a new and consciously ecclesial theology. It was not for nothing that his great work of dogmatic theology was published under the title of *Church Dogmatics*. The youth movement now being formed was also the bearer of a new discovery of the liturgy. Under the sign of this awareness, the denominations now also came to a new rapprochement, to a passionate search for the *Una Sancta*. Schmaus had written his dogmatics in this spirit. Egenter, the moral theologian, along with others (above all Fritz Tillmann and Theodor Stein-büchel), represented the tendency to seek a new form for moral theology, a desire to end the dominance of casuistry and the natural law and to rethink morality on the basis of the following of Christ.

Next to the exegetes, however, those who had the greatest influence over me were Söhngen and Pascher. Söhngen had originally wanted to be only a philosopher and had begun his career with a dissertation on Kant. He belonged to that dynamic current in Thomism that took from Thomas the passion for truth and the habit of asking unrelenting questions about the foundation and goal of all the real; but all of this he consciously placed in relation to the questions that philosophy asks today. With his phenomenology, Husserl had opened the door for metaphysics at least a crack, a door others were now throwing wide open, although in very different ways. Heidegger was asking questions concerning being, Scheler concerning values, and Nikolai Hartmann was attempting to develop a metaphysics in a rigorously Aristotelian spirit. External circumstances directed Söhngen toward theology. Being the child of a mixed marriage and deeply concerned with the ecumenical question on account of his origins, Söhngen took up the debate with Karl Barth and Emil Brunner. He also ventured out with great competence into the mystery theology founded by Odo Casel, the Benedictine monk from Maria Laach. This theology had grown directly out of the liturgical movement, and its very existence posed with new acuteness the basic question concerning the relationship between rationality and mystery, the question concerning the place of the Platonic and the philosophical in Christianity, and, indeed, the question about the essence of Christianity. Characteristic of Söhngen above all was the fact that he always developed his thought on the basis of the sources themselves, beginning with Aristotle and Plato, then on to Clement of Alexandria and Augustine, Anselm, Bonaventure, and Thomas, all the way to Luther and finally the Tübingen theologians of the last century. Pascal and Newman, too, were among his favorite authors. What particularly impressed me about him was that he was never satisfied in theology with the sort of positivism that could usually be detected in other subjects. Rather, he always asked the question concerning the truth of the matter and hence the question concerning the immediate reality of what is believed.

Pascher, the pastoral theologian, was also, as I have said, the director of our Georgianum. He often struck our hearts directly in his lively spiritual conferences, in which he spoke to us, very personally and without any of the usual clichés, out of his own rich spiritual experience. In his system of education everything rested on the daily celebration of Holy Mass. He opened up to us the nature and structure of the Mass in a series of lectures in the summer of 1948, which had already appeared in book form in 1947 under the title *Eucharistia*. Until this time I had had my reservations about the liturgical movement. In many of its representatives I sensed a one-sided rationalism and historicism that concentrated too much on forms and historical origins and exhibited a remarkable coldness when it came to dispositions of mind and heart that allow us to experience the Church as the place where the soul is at home. To be sure, my *Schott* was a precious possession to me, indeed, something irreplaceable; the unquestionably positive gain of the liturgical movement was the way in which this missal made the liturgy accessible and encouraged its celebration in a manner befitting its nature. But I was bothered by the narrow-mindedness of many of the movement's followers, who wanted to recognize only *one* form of the liturgy as valid.

Pascher's conferences, and the reverential manner in which he taught us to celebrate the liturgy in keeping with its deepest nature, made me a follower of the liturgical movement. Just as I learned to understand the New Testament as being the soul of all theology, so too I came to see the liturgy as being its living element, without which it would necessarily shrivel up. This is why, at the beginning of the Council, I saw that the draft of the Constitution on the Liturgy, which incorporated all the essential principles of the liturgical movement, was a marvelous point of departure for this assembly of the whole Church, and I advised Cardinal Frings in this sense. I was not able to foresee that the negative sides of the liturgical movement would afterward reemerge with redoubled strength, almost to the point of pushing the liturgy toward its own self-destruction.

When I look back on the exciting years of my theological studies, I can only be amazed at everything that is affirmed nowadays concerning the "preconciliar" Church. All of us lived with a feeling of radical change that had already arisen in the 1920s, the sense of a theology that had the courage to ask new questions and a spirituality that was doing away with what was dusty and obsolete and leading to a new joy in the redemption. Dogma was conceived, not as an external shackle, but as the living source that made knowledge of the truth possible in the first place. The Church came to life for us above all in the liturgy and in the great richness of the theological tradition. We did not take the demands of celibacy lightly, but we were convinced that we did well to trust the Church's experience of many centuries and that the deep-reaching renunciation she required of us would bear fruit. While in Catholic Germany at that time one could generally count on a joyful enthusiasm for the papacy and a heartfelt veneration for the great figure of Pius XII, the atmosphere in the theological faculty was a few degrees cooler. The theology we were learning was to a large extent by the historical method, so that the style of the Roman pronouncements, couched more in the neoscholastic tradition, had a foreign sound to us. Perhaps German arrogance also contributed a little to our belief that we knew what was what better than "those down there". The experiences of our respected teacher Maier made us doubt the appropriateness of many a Roman decision, especially since the two-source theory, which had been rejected previously, had now become a commonplace. But such reservations and sentiments did not for a moment diminish the deep assent of our faith to the primacy in the form in which the First Vatican Council had defined it.

In this connection I would like to relate a small episode that I think can cast much light on the situation. Before Mary's bodily Assumption into heaven was defined, all theological faculties in the world were consulted for their opinion. Our teachers' answer was emphatically negative. What here became evident was the one-sidedness, not only of the historical, but also of the historicist method in theology. "Tradition" was identified with what could be proved on the basis of texts. Altaner, the patrologist from Würzburg (who also had come from Breslau), had proven in a scientifically persuasive manner that the doctrine of Mary's bodily Assumption into heaven was unknown before the fifth century; this doctrine, therefore, he argued, could not belong to the "apostolic tradition". And this was his conclusion, which my teachers at Munich shared. This argument is compelling if you understand "tradition" strictly as the handing down of fixed formulas and texts. This was the position that our teachers represented. But if you conceive of "tradition" as the living process whereby the Holy Spirit introduces us to the fullness of truth and teaches us how to understand what previously we could still not grasp (cf. Jn 16:12–13), then subsequent "remembering" (cf. Jn 16:4, for instance) can come to recognize what it had not caught sight of previously and yet was already handed down in the original Word. But such a perspective was still quite unattainable by German theological thought. In 1949, I think, Gottlieb Söhngen held forth passionately against the possibility of this Marian dogma before the circle for ecumenical dialogue presided over by Archbishop Jäger, of Paderborn, and Lutheran Bishop Stählin (the circle out of which the *Einheitsrat,* or "Council for Unity", developed later on). In response, Edmund Schlink, a Lutheran expert in systematic theology from Heidelberg, asked Söhngen point-blank: "But what will you do if the dogma is nevertheless defined? Won't you then have to turn your back on the Catholic Church?" After reflecting for a moment, Söhngen answered: "If the dogma comes, then I will remember that the Church is wiser than I and that I must trust her more than my own erudition." I think that this small scene says everything about the spirit in which theology was done here—both critically and with faith.

In the fall of 1949 a wing of the Georgianum on Ludwig-straße in Munich was finally made halfway habitable, and also the number of lecture halls in the university across the street increased to the point that we could return to the city. We saw at once that much remained to be done. Access to our living quarters on the fourth floor still led through an outdoor area and, at the very beginning, up a ladder. Now it was at last possible to attend lectures in other faculties, although the approaching period of final examinations set clear limits to our desires. What we gained by living in the city and being able to work within a complete university was undeniable; but I also perceived clearly what was lost. In Fürstenried all of us—teachers, seminarians, and students of both sexes who came out from the city—had lived together like one big family. Such a sense of immediacy and nearness was now missing. Thus, the Fürstenried years remain in my memory as a time of great awakening, full of hope and trust, as well as a time of great and difficult decisions. When I occasionally walk again in the castle park, which has remained unchanged, its gravel paths so become one with the interior ones I walked there that everything from those days is again present before me, fresh and unspoiled.

The house in which Joseph Ratzinger was born on April 16, 1927. The plaque notes the place and birth date of the "then archbishop of Munich-Freising".

The town of Marktl am Inn, the place of Ratzinger's birth, on the border between Bavaria and Austria.

TOP The Ratzinger family—parents, Joseph and Maria, older brother, Georg, sister, Maria, and young Joseph (on the left).

RIGHT Brothers Georg and Joseph Ratzinger, with their friend Rupert Berger between them, on the day of their ordination to the priesthood on June 29, 1951, being welcomed for celebrations in Traunstein, where their parents had settled.

ABOVE The Ratzinger family after the first Mass
of the two brothers (July 8, 1951).

RIGHT Ratzinger as young professor of fundamental theology in Bonn (1961).

BELOW Ratzinger's parents, with his brother, Georg, in front of the house in
Hufschlag near Traunstein, in the fall of 1955.

LEFT   Ratzinger as advisor at Vatican Council II (fall 1964).

BELOW   Ratzinger in conversation with Karl Rahner (on the left) and his student Fr. Martin Bialas in the Benedictine abbey of Weltenburg (February 1977).

RIGHT Ratzinger's episcopal coat of arms, with the motto *Cooperatores veritatis* (Co-workers of the Truth, from 3 John 8), which signifies the interweaving of truth and love, of personal faith and the catholicity of the Church, as well as the interrelationship of ministers and faithful, who, in their different ways, share together the burden and grace of the Gospel.

BELOW Official photo in the archbishop's palace in Munich (spring 1978).

ABOVE With Pope John Paul II, on the occasion of the latter's first trip to Germany (November 1980).

RIGHT Meeting with artists and intellectuals during the Pope's visit to Munich.

Cardinal Ratzinger, as Prefect of the Congregation for the Doctrine of the Faith, at the signing of the Apostolic Constitution that promulgated the new Code of Canon Law (Vatican City, January 25, 1983).

LEFT   The Cardinal presides at the
solemn vespers of Epiphany in the
Church of St. Peter, Munich
(January 6, 1996).

BELOW   Participating in the procession
of Palm Sunday in St. Peter's Square,
Vatican City (March 31, 1985).

Trip to Peru (July 17–26, 1986).

ABOVE Arrival at the Airport of Cuzco, the famous capital city of the Inca kingdom. Cardinal Ratzinger is welcomed by the Archbishop, His Excellency Alcides Mendoza Castro (July 22, 1986).

BELOW Greeting of the authorities and others present.

ABOVE   With a group of faithful to whom Cardinal Ratzinger administered Holy Confirmation.

RIGHT   Visit to a family in Cuzco.

BELOW   With the faithful in front of the Cathedral in Cuzco (July 22, 1986).

LEFT, ABOVE   Visit to Sacsayhuamán (July 22, 1986), accompanied by the nuncio, His Excellency Luigi Dossena.

LEFT, BELOW   Visit to Machu Picchu.

ABOVE   High in the Andes, Machu Picchu (July 23, 1986).

Celebration on the occasion of Cardinal Ratzinger's sixtieth birthday.

LEFT   Cardinal Ratzinger in his office (September 29, 1986).
[Photo by J. H. Darchinger.]

FOLLOWING PAGES   In the Plaza of Saint Peter, the Cardinal walks to his office
(October 29, 1993).

LEFT   During visit to Domaine "La Bergerie", Upper Savoy (September 1988). The Cardinal plays the piano, a family passion.

RIGHT AND BELOW   Picnic with friends in the park of Valle del Treja (Rome, May 13, 1990).

Tenth anniversary of the pontificate of John Paul II (October 30, 1988).

ABOVE   Cardinal Ratzinger presides at the Eucharist.

RIGHT   During his homily.

BELOW   He receives the greeting of the Pope after the celebration.

During summertime at his house in Pentling (Regensburg),
with his sister, Maria.

ABOVE   Teatime.

RIGHT   Moments of reflection and relaxation in the tree-lined garden that
surrounds the house.

ABOVE   Cardinal Ratzinger
with his brother, Georg, and his
sister, Maria, in front of the
Cathedral of Bressanone
(September 30, 1990).

LEFT   With his sister, Maria, at
the door of his house in Rome
(May 1990).

RIGHT, ABOVE   The Cardinal at
his desk in the Congregation.

RIGHT, BOTTOM   Together with
Cardinal Bernard Law, Archbishop of Boston, member of
the preparatory commission of
the *Catechism*, the Cardinal
presents the English edition of
the *Catechism of the Catholic
Church* to the Pope at Gemeli
General Hospital (May 27,
1994).

Cardinal Ratzinger during an interview in the audience hall of the
Congregation for the Doctrine of the Faith.

In Paris, Cardinal Ratzinger is welcomed
among the members of the Institut de France,
"Académie des Sciences morales et politiques" (November 7, 1992).

ABOVE AND BELOW   During the initiation ceremony.

RIGHT   Commemorative speech on Andrei Sacharov, whom Ratzinger
succeeded as a member of the French Academy.

ABOVE   Visiting Paestum with his brother, Georg (June 10, 1995).

RIGHT   On the airplane with Pope John Paul II, on the occasion of the latter's third trip to Germany (June 21, 1996).

FOLLOWING PAGES   Cardinal Ratzinger in the archives of the Congregation (October 21, 1993). [Photo by Gianni Giansanti.]

7

Priestly Ordination—
Ministry—Doctorate

After the final examination in theology in the summer of
1950, an unexpected assignment came my way that once
again made my life change tracks decisively. In the theological faculty there was a custom every year for an open
competition to be held involving a written assignment that
had to be completed within nine months and handed in
anonymously under a code name. If one of the works received the prize (which consisted of a very modest sum of
money), then it was automatically accepted as a dissertation
with the mention *Summa cum laude*. The winner, thus, had
the door to the doctorate opened before him. Every year a
different professor formulated the assignment, so that the
different theological disciplines were covered one by one.
During the month of July, Gottlieb Söhngen told me that
this year he was responsible for determining the theme and
that he was counting on my willingness to enter the competition. I felt duty-bound, and I looked forward with
excitement to the moment when the theme would be pub-
licly announced. The subject chosen by the professor was:
"The People and the House of God in Augustine's Doctrine
of the Church". Since in recent years I had been zealously
reading the Fathers and had also taken Söhngen's seminar on
Augustine, I felt I could set out on this adventure.

Another circumstance came to my aid. In the fall of 1949, Alfred Läpple had given me *Catholicism,* perhaps Henri de Lubac's most significant work, in the masterful translation by Hans Urs von Balthasar. This book was for me a key reading event. It gave me not only a new and deeper connection with the thought of the Fathers but also a new way of looking at theology and faith as such. Faith had here become an interior contemplation and, precisely by thinking with the Fathers, a present reality. In this book one could detect a quiet debate going on with both liberalism and Marxism, the dramatic struggle of French Catholicism for a new penetration of the faith into the intellectual life of our time. De Lubac was leading his readers out of a narrowly individualistic and moralistic mode of faith and into the freedom of an essentially social faith, conceived and lived as a *we*—a faith that, precisely as such and according to its nature, was also hope, affecting history as a whole, and not only the promise of a private blissfulness to individuals. I then looked around for other works by de Lubac and derived special profit from his book *Corpus Mysticum,* in which a new understanding of the unity of Church and Eucharist opened up to me beyond the insights I had already received from Pascher, Schmaus, and Söhngen. Drawing on these perspectives, I could now enter into the required dialogue with Augustine, something I had already been attempting for a long time in different ways.

The long vacation period that lasted from the end of July to the end of October was completely given over to my competition essay. But then a difficult situation came into being. At the end of October we received ordination to the subdiaconate and to the diaconate. With this began in earnest the preparation for priestly ordination, which at that time was somewhat different from today. Now we were all together again in the seminary in Freising and were being introduced to the practical aspects of the priestly ministry; among other things, we had to be trained in homiletics and catechesis. The seriousness of this preparation demanded the whole person, without any reservation, and yet I had to try to combine it with the writing of my theme. The tolerance of the house and the consideration of my colleagues made this difficult combination possible. My brother, who was with me on the road to the priesthood, did everything possible to relieve me of all practical tasks relating to our preparation for priestly ordination and our first Mass. My sister, who at this time was working as a secretary in a legal firm, used her free time to produce in exemplary fashion a clean copy of the manuscript, and so I was able to hand in my work by the required deadline.

I was very happy when I was finally free of such an engaging and yet burdensome task, and I could now dedicate myself completely for at least the last two months to preparing for the big step: ordination to the priesthood, which Cardinal Faulhaber would confer on us in the cathedral at Freising on the Feast of Saints Peter and Paul in 1951. We were more than forty candidates, who, at the solemn call on that radiant summer day, which I remember as the high point of my life, responded *"Adsum"*, Here I am. We should not be superstitious; but, at the moment when the elderly archbishop laid his hands on me, a little bird—perhaps a lark—flew up from the high altar in the cathedral and trilled a little joyful song. And I could not but see in this a reassurance from on high, as if I heard the words "This is good, you are on the right way." There then followed four summer weeks that were like an unending feast. On the day of our first Holy Mass, our parish church of Saint Oswald gleamed in all its splendor, and the joy that almost palpably filled the whole place drew everyone there into the most living mode of "active participation" in the sacred event, but this did not require any external busyness. We were invited to bring the first blessing into people's homes, and everywhere we were received even by total strangers with a warmth and affection I had not thought possible until that day. In this way I learned firsthand how earnestly people wait for a priest, how much they long for the blessing that flows from the power of the sacrament. The point was not my own or my brother's person. What could we two young men represent all by ourselves to the many people we were now meeting? In us they saw persons who had been touched by Christ's mission and had been empowered to bring his nearness to men. Precisely because we ourselves were not the point, a friendly human relationship could develop very quickly.

Made strong by the experience of these weeks, on August 1 I began my ministry as assistant pastor in the parish of the Precious Blood in Munich. The greater portion of the parish lay in a residential suburb in which intellectuals, artists, and high government officials lived; but there were also rows of houses belonging to employees and people who worked in small shops, as well as butlers and maids, who in those days belonged to the wealthier households. The rectory had been built by a famous architect. It was homey but too small, and the great number of people who came to help out in various functions often created a hectic atmosphere. But the important thing was my encounter with the pastor, good Father Blumschein, who not only said to others that a priest had to "glow" but was himself a person who glowed within. To his last breath he desired with every fiber of his being to offer priestly service. He died, in fact, bringing the sacraments to a dying person. His kindness and inner fervor for his priestly mission were what gave a special character to this rectory.

What at first glance could appear to be hectic activity was in reality the expression of a continually lived readiness to serve.

I surely was in need of such a model, because the load of tasks assigned to me was great. I had to give sixteen hours of religious instruction at five different levels, which obviously required much preparation. Every Sunday I had to celebrate at least two Masses and give two different sermons. Every morning I sat in the confessional from six to seven, and on Saturday afternoons for four hours. Every week there were several burials in the various cemeteries of the city. I was totally responsible for youth ministry, and to this I had to add extracurricular obligations like baptisms, weddings, and so on. Since the pastor did not spare himself, neither did I want to, nor could I spare myself. Because of my scant practical training, I had at first some difficulty with these duties. But soon the work with the children in the school, and the resulting association with their parents, became a great joy to me, and the encounter with different groups of Catholic youth also quickly generated a good feeling of community. To be sure, it also became evident how far removed the world of the life and thinking of many children was from the realities of faith and how little our religious instruction coincided with the actual lives and thinking of our families. Nor could I overlook the fact that the form of youth work, which was simply a continuation of methods developed between the two World Wars, would not be able to deal with the changing circumstances of the world we now lived in: we simply had to look for new forms. Some of the insights that came to me as I experienced these changed conditions I gathered up some years later in my essay "The New Pagans and the Church", which at that time triggered a lively discussion.

My assignment to the seminary in Freising, which my superiors decided would begin on October 1, 1952, aroused various reactions in me. On the one hand, this was the solution I had desired, the one that would enable me to return to my theological work, which I loved so much. On the other hand, I suffered a great deal, especially in the first year, from the loss of all the human contacts and experiences afforded me by the pastoral ministry. In fact, I even began to think I would have done better to remain in parish work. The feeling of being needed and of accomplishing an important service had helped me to give all I could, and this gave me a joy in the priesthood that I did not experience in so direct a manner in my new assignment. I now had to give a series of lectures to the last-year students on the pastoral aspects of the sacraments, and, although the experience I could draw on was rather limited, at least it was recent and fresh in my mind. To this was added work in the cathedral—liturgical services and hours in the confessional—as well as the responsibility of a youth group started by my predecessor. Above all I had to complete my doctorate, which at that time was no mean proposition: in each of eight subjects I had to pass a one-hour oral examination and complete a written examination, and the process culminated in an open debate for which I had to prepare theses from all theological disciplines. Especially for Father and Mother, it was a great joy when, in July 1953, I walked across the stage and received the cap as doctor of theology.

8

The Drama of My *Habilitation*[*] and the Freising Years

It so happened that precisely at the end of the summer semester of 1953, the chair for dogmatic and fundamental theology at the College [*Hochschule*] for Philosophy and Theology in Freising was vacated. For one year it had been occupied by Otfried Müller, a priest from Silesia, who was trying simultaneously to advance the work for his *habilitation*—truly a difficult undertaking, considering the demands of teaching two core theological courses. Now the Theological College at Erfurt, interested in faculty development, had asked Müller to take over their dogmatics chair. It was no easy decision to move from the upward-bound West of Germany, with its high standard of living and its freedom, over to the Soviet-occupied sector of our homeland, which at that time even more than later gave the impression of being one huge prison. Müller accepted the call and proceeded to form a whole generation of priests in the German Democratic Republic. The body of professors at the college in Freising let it be known that they were thinking of me as

* The *habilitation* is the degree that qualifies a person to hold a chair at a German university. It is obtained by writing a weighty scholarly book that proposes and defends a thesis and then receiving approval for it from an academic committee.—Trans.

successor to Müller; but I wanted to spend at least another year in the position I had at the seminary because, despite the bundle of duties it brought with it, it still left me considerably more leisure to prepare my *habilitation* than would have been the case with the position offered me at the college. Father Viktor Schurr, a dogma expert from the Redemptorist college in Gars, a cheerful and intelligent priest from Swabia, therefore took over the chair in Freising for one year, in the course of which we developed a good friendship.

My first concern was to determine the theme for my *habilitation*. Gottlieb Söhngen decided that, now that my work in patristic theology was concluded, I should turn to the Middle Ages. Since I had just done work on Augustine, it seemed natural for me to work on Bonaventure, whose theology had occupied Söhngen rather intensely. And since the dissertation had dealt with an ecclesiological theme, I was now to turn to the other great thematic area of fundamental theology, namely, the concept of revelation. At this time the idea of salvation history had moved to the focus of inquiry posed by Catholic theology, and this had cast new light on the notion of revelation, which neoscholasticism had kept too confined to the intellectual realm. Revelation now appeared no longer simply as a communication of truths to the intellect but as a historical action of God in which truth becomes gradually unveiled. Therefore, I was to try to discover whether in Bonaventure there was anything corresponding to the concept of salvation history, and whether this motif—if it should exist—had any relationship with the idea of revelation. I went to work with both zeal and joy. Although I had some rudimentary knowledge of Bonaventure and had already read some of his shorter writings, new worlds opened up as I made progress with my work. When Father Schurr packed his things and took his leave in the summer of 1954, I had already completed gathering materials and had also worked out the basic outline for the interpretation of what I had found; but the difficult job of actually writing the book still stood before me.

Once again something remarkable happened. Because of the death of a retired philosophy professor of the college, one of the residences for professors up on the Domberg became available, and I was urged to move into this house and set up a household at the same time as I took over the chair for dogma. But all of this was happening too fast for me, especially since I still had to do the main part of the work for my *habilitation*. I did, in fact, assume the chair for dogma and begin lecturing in the winter semester; but I was allowed to postpone fundamental theology for another year. I began with a series of lectures on God four hours per week; it was a joy to move through this great question and the richness of the tradition concerning it. The enthusiasm of the students helped me to combine the double work of the lectures and of the writing of the book for my *habilitation*. By the end of the summer semester of 1955, the handwritten manuscript was ready. Unfortunately I hit upon a typist who was not only slow but who now and then also lost pages and taxed my nerves to the utmost by committing all manner of errors, particularly in connection with the page numbers in the references. The battle to discover and correct all the mistakes sometimes seemed almost endless. Late in the fall I was finally able to hand in the two prescribed copies to the faculty in Munich. I was anything but happy with their printed appearance, but at least I could hope that no glaring errors had remained in the text.

In the meantime, the question of the house was coming to a head. My father was now seventy-eight years old and my mother seventy-one, so for my parents the originally idyllic situation in Hufschlag was becoming more arduous. The church and all shops were located in the city of Traunstein, which always meant a two-kilometer walk, and this was no easy thing, especially in the Traunstein winters, with huge amounts of snow and often frozen streets. As attached as we all were to the quiet house at the edge of the forest, the moment seemed to have arrived to look for a new solution. Since my *habilitation* appeared assured and the house on the Domberg still awaited new tenants, it seemed to all of us that the right thing to do was to bring Father and Mother to Freising. In this way they would be living next to the cathedral, the shops would be nearby, and we could once again bring the family together; and my sister, too, was thinking of joining us a bit later on. The move took place on November 17, a very foggy day whose melancholy affected my dear parents in the hour of a farewell that meant leaving behind not only a place but a part of their life. But they set out with courage and vigor. Barely had the movers arrived when Mother put on her apron to lend a hand, and by evening she was already at the stove preparing the first meal. Father was likewise full of attentiveness and energy, helping everything run smoothly. A whole crowd of students also came and were busy doing every conceivable thing, and this was a great encouragement, because we were not walking into an empty space but into a network of friendship and mutual affection. That year we experienced a very happy Advent, and, when my brother and sister also joined us at Christmas, the strange new house again became a real home.

None of us suspected at this time what stormy clouds hung over me. Gottlieb Söhngen had immediately read my *habilitation* thesis; he had accepted it enthusiastically and even quoted from it frequently in his lectures. Professor Schmaus, the other reader, was a very busy man, and so he left the manuscript untouched for a couple of months. From a secretary I found out that he had finally begun reading it in February. At Easter of 1956 he put out a call to all German-speaking experts in dogma for the purpose of holding a congress in Königstein; this was the origin of the Working Community of German Dogmatists and Fundamental Theologians, which still meets regularly. I, too, was present, and this was incidentally the occasion when I first met Karl Rahner personally. He was in the midst of editing a new edition of the *Lexikon für Theologie und Kirche,* founded by Bishop Buchberger, and, since I had to write some articles for the parallel Lutheran work, *Die Religion in Geschichte und Gegenwart,* Rahner questioned me with interest about the editorial methods this publication employed. So it was that already on this first occasion we developed a very warm personal relationship. During the Königstein congress Schmaus called me aside for a brief private conversation, during which he told me very directly and without emotion that he had to reject my *habilitation* thesis because it did not meet the pertinent scholarly standards. I would learn details after the appropriate decision by the faculty. I was thunderstruck. A whole world was threatening to collapse around me. What was to become of my parents, who in good faith had come to me in Freising, if I now had to leave the college because of my failure? And all of my future plans would likewise collapse, since these, too, were all contingent on my being a professor of theology. I thought of applying for the position of assistant pastor in the parish of Saint Georg in Freising, which came with a house; but this solution was not particularly consoling.

The only thing to do in the meantime was wait, and so it was with a hollow feeling that I embarked on the summer semester. What had happened? As far as I can piece things together, there were three contributing factors. In my research I had seen that the study of the Middle Ages in Munich, primarily represented by Michael Schmaus, had come to almost a complete halt at its prewar state. The great new breakthroughs that had been made in the meantime, particularly by those writing in French, had not even been acknowledged. With a forthrightness not advisable in a beginner, I criticized the superseded positions, and this was apparently too much for Schmaus, especially since it was unthinkable to him that I could have worked on a medieval theme without entrusting myself to his direction. The copy of my book that he used was in the end full of glosses of all colors in the margins, which themselves left nothing to be desired by way of forthrightness. And while he was at it, he expressed irritation at the deficient appearance of the graphic layout and at various errors in the references that had remained despite all my efforts.

But he also did not like the result of my analyses. I had ascertained that in Bonaventure (as well as in theologians of the thirteenth century) there was nothing corresponding to our conception of "revelation", by which we are normally in the habit of referring to all the revealed contents of the faith: it has even become a part of linguistic usage to refer to Sacred Scripture simply as "revelation". Such an identification would have been unthinkable in the language of the High Middle Ages. Here, "revelation" is always a concept denoting an act. The word refers to the act in which God shows himself, not to the objectified result of this act. And because this is so, the receiving subject is always also a part of the concept of "revelation". Where there is no one to perceive "revelation", no re-*vel*-ation has occurred, because no *veil* has been removed. By definition, revelation requires a someone who apprehends it. These insights, gained through my reading of Bonaventure, were later on very important for me at the time of the conciliar discussion on revelation, Scripture, and tradition. Because, if Bonaventure is right, then revelation precedes Scripture and becomes deposited in Scripture but is not simply identical with it. This in turn means that revelation is always something greater than what is merely written down. And this again means that there can be no such thing as pure *sola scriptura* ("by Scripture alone"), because an essential element of Scripture is the Church as understanding subject, and with this the fundamental sense of tradition is already given. At that moment, however, the burning question was the *habilitation* thesis, and Michael Schmaus, who had perhaps also heard annoying rumors from some in Freising concerning the modernity of my theology, saw in these theses not at all a faithful rendering of Bonaventure's thought (however, to this day I still affirm the contrary) but a dangerous modernism that had to lead to the subjectivization of the concept of revelation.

At the faculty meeting that dealt with my *habilitation* thesis, things most likely got rather stormy. Unlike Söhngen, Schmaus could count on strong friends in the body of professors, and yet the damning sentence was softened. The work was not rejected but given back for revision. I was supposed to figure out what was to be improved from the marginal comments that Schmaus had scribbled in his copy. This gave me hope again, even if, as Professor Söhngen informed me, Schmaus had blurted out after the decision that the extent of the needed reworking was so great that years would be required. In that case, a rejection would have amounted to the same thing, and I would have doubtless had to give up my work in the college. I thumbed through the badly disfigured copy of my book and made an encouraging discovery: While the first two parts were swarming with critical notations that I found only rarely persuasive and that were sometimes cleared up two pages later, the last part (on Bonaventure's theology of history) had remained free of all objections. And yet precisely this part was a potential minefield. What exactly was happening?

The Franciscan movement had early on become aware of the fact that its development had certain peculiar connections with the historical prophecies of Joachim of Fiore, a southern Italian abbot who had died in 1202. This pious scholar believed that he could interpret Scripture to mean that history would develop from a stern Kingdom of the Father (Old Testament) to the Kingdom of the Son (the Church until that moment) to a third Kingdom, the Kingdom of the Spirit, in which the promises of the prophets would finally be fulfilled and nothing but freedom and love would reign. Joachim believed that in the Bible he had also found a basis for reckoning the time when the Church of the Spirit would emerge, and these calculations suggested that Francis of Assisi should be seen as the beginning of the new era and his community of brothers as the bearers of this new age. Already toward the middle of the thirteenth century, radical interpretations of this idea were made that finally drove the so-called "spirituals" out of the Order and into open conflict with the papacy. In a late two-volume work, Henri de Lubac has studied the subsequent history of Joachim's idea, which reaches out to Hegel and the totalitarian systems of our own century. Now, it had always been said that Bonaventure never quoted Joachim, and the name "Joachim" could not be found in the critical edition of his works. When examined, this thesis was bound to seem questionable because, as general of his Order, Bonaventure was inevitably thrown into the controversy concerning the relationship between Francis and Joachim. In the end he had to put his predecessor, John of Parma—who was saintly but much inclined to Joachim's ideas—into a monastic prison in order to forestall the polarization that might have been supported by the pious man. In my work I was the first to show that, in his interpretation of the "six days of creation", Bonaventure had debated Joachim's ideas extensively and, as a man of the center, had striven to keep what was useful in order to integrate it into the ecclesial order. This result of my research was understandably not received by all with enthusiasm at first, but it has become the standard view in the meantime. As I have said, Schmaus made no criticism at all of this part of my work.

An idea then came to the rescue. What I had said about Bonaventure's theology of history was certainly interwoven with the whole of my book, and yet it could largely stand on its own. Without much difficulty, it could be detached from the work and reshaped to form a whole. In a volume of some two hundred pages, such a book would indeed be shorter than had become customary for *habilitation* theses, and yet it would be long enough to demonstrate the author's ability to do independent theological research, which was the whole point of the undertaking. Since, despite the sharp criticism of my work, this part had passed through without objections, it could surely not be declared subsequently to be scientifically unacceptable. I presented my idea to Gottlieb Söhngen, and at once he agreed. Unfortunately, my calendar for the long vacation period was mostly full, but I was still able to free up two weeks to complete the necessary reworking. And so, already in October, I was able to put the rejected opus back on the table in abridged form, much to the faculty's astonishment. Once again weeks of restless waiting followed. Finally, on February 11, 1957, I learned that my *habilitation* thesis had been accepted, and the public lecture connected with this event was scheduled for February 21. According to the rules for *habilitation* then in force in Munich, this lecture and the disputation following it still belonged to the requirements for *habilitation*, which meant that it was possible to fail here too, this time in public—and this had in fact happened twice already after the war. So I was not wholly carefree as the day drew near, since my time to prepare was short on account of my continuing lectures in Freising. The large auditorium chosen for the occasion was full to overflowing, and an extraordinary tension was almost palpable in the air. After my presentation, both official readers had to make their comments. Before long the discussion with me had become a passionate disputation between the two of them. They would turn to the public and hold forth their views, while I stood in the background unrequired. The subsequent deliberation by the faculty lasted a long time. Finally, the dean came out into the hallway where I was waiting with my brother and my friends and announced to me without ceremony that I had passed and was now in possession of my *habilitation*.

At the moment I could hardly feel any joy, so heavily did the nightmare of what had happened weigh me down. But slowly the anxiety that had taken root in me began to dissolve; I could now carry on with my service in Freising in peace, without having to harbor the fear that I had pushed my parents into a sad adventure. Soon afterward I was named a lecturer [*Privatdozent*] at the University of Munich, and on January 1, 1958—not without some sniper shots from certain disgruntled quarters—I was named professor of fundamental theology and dogma at the College of Philosophy and Theology in Freising. My relationship with Professor Schmaus understandably remained tense at first, but then in the 1970s things eased up, and we became friends. I still could not accept his judgments and decisions of the time as having been scientifically justified, but I realized that the trials of that difficult year were healthy for me humanly speaking and that, so to speak, they were following a logic higher than the merely scientific one. At first, the distance to Schmaus resulted in my coming closer to Karl Rahner. Above all, however, I made the resolve not to agree easily to the rejection of dissertations or *habilitation* theses but whenever possible—and respecting the integrity of the procedure—to take the side of the weaker party. This attitude would later on play a role in my academic career, as we will see.

Before long I was again facing new decisions and also new hardships. Already in the summer of 1956, at the height of the quarrel over my *habilitation*, a preliminary feeler had been put out to me by the dean of the Catholic Theological Faculty in Mainz, inquiring whether I was interested in taking over their chair in fundamental theology. I immediately said no, for one thing because I could not do this to my parents, and then, too, because I did not want to walk away from the fight over my *habilitation* as a deserter, so to speak, someone who could in the future be branded as a failure. Now, in the summer of 1958, I was being invited to the chair in fundamental theology in Bonn, the very chair that my teacher Söhngen had always wanted for himself but that had remained closed to him given the academy's political configuration in those days. For me, going there was like a dream come true. In contrast to 1956, the situation in respect to the two reasons for not leaving Freising had now changed.

Again something had happened that I could only see as a providential disposition. My brother, who had continued to study music alongside his pastoral duties, in 1957 concluded his studies with the master class at the Munich College of Music. Now he was assigned to the position of choir director in our home parish of Saint Oswald in Traunstein. With this came the responsibility for musical education at the Traunstein minor seminary, and he would also engage in pastoral work. As benefice for celebrating early Mass, he was given as a residence the attractive little house in which until now the preacher in the parish church had lodged. The house was located right in the middle of the city; it was quiet and lovely and had as much space as our former home in Hufschlag. Although until now it had seemed impossible for our parents to move again, a return to their unforgettable and still beloved Traunstein was conceivable. I discussed the matter first with my brother, who was all for my going to Bonn and was more than happy to receive our parents at his house. Next we had to win over Father, who did not find it altogether easy to agree, although he did clearly want me to take advantage of the opportunity that was being offered me. Unfortunately, we informed Mother too late, since we did not want to make her needlessly anxious, and she learned what was happening from a third party. For long afterward she suffered from what she perceived had been a lack of trust on our part. And so another portion of our life concluded. Once again I had been granted the possibility of living with my dear parents, and in their gentle company I had found the sense of shelter that was precisely what I so needed during the turbulent events I had to undergo. The Domberg in Freising, where at present there is unfortunately no seminary, became like a second home to me. The memories it evokes bring before my mind's eye both the important (if also endangered) beginning of my career and the images of everyday life together and the festive hours we were given to experience there.

9

Professorship in Bonn

On April 15, 1959, I began my lectures as ordinary professor of fundamental theology at the University of Bonn. The large lecture hall was very full, and my listeners reacted enthusiastically to the new tone they thought they could hear in my words. For the time being I still lived at the Albertinum, the residence for theological students, and this was very good at the beginning. This enabled me to participate in the ordinary day-to-day existence of the "theologians", and so I quickly developed an easy rapport with my students. Both the city and the university excited me. The Hofgarten, through which I had to walk to the nearby university, was all aglow that sunny year with the full splendor of spring. The university still showed the wounds of the war, which could be seen especially in the gaps in the university library and in the seminary libraries, whose large collections of sources—which I so needed for my work—were still incomplete. But the noble structure of the old electoral residence, which after the end of the Napoleonic era had become the main building of the university, had not lost its special atmosphere even as a result of the war. The academic life that pulsed there, the encounter with students and professors of all faculties, really excited and inspired me. At night I could hear the whistles on the Rhine, which flows by the Albertinum. The great river with its international shipping traffic gave me the feeling of openness and breadth, of the meeting of cultures and nations that for centuries had occurred here and made one another fruitful. While Bavaria is a land of farmers and owes its special beauty, permanence, and inner peace precisely to this characteristic, I now found myself in a landscape with a wholly different quality about it. Cologne was close, Aachen not far, Düsseldorf and the Ruhr region belonged to the area drained by this same Rhine. In addition, we had a whole series of theological colleges around us: in Walberberg, the Dominicans' house of studies; in Hennef-Geistingen, that of the Redemptorists, with a very beautiful and well-cared-for library; in Sankt Augustin, the Divine Word (or "Steyler") Missionaries had an important institute for the missions; in Mönchengladbach, there were the Franciscans, and among them Sophronius Clasen, the great Bonaventure specialist, whose friend I soon became.

Here fresh impulses came from everywhere, especially since Belgium and the Netherlands were near and the Rhineland has traditionally been the gate to France. All on its own, a circle of interested students quickly started to form with whom I would hold regular colloquia, a tradition I continued until 1993, obviously with changing participants! The Catholic theological faculty had outstanding professors in many of its disciplines. Theodor Klauser, the founder and editor of the *Reallexikon für Antike und Christentum,* was a prominent figure. Hubert Jedin, the great historian of the Council of Trent, soon became my personal friend, and I was very close to him until his death in 1980. Schöllgen, the moral theologian, had a universal education that made him a most stimulating conversationalist. I could continue this list but will only add that having several Bavarian colleagues working in Bonn with me quite soon made me feel at home.

The dogma specialist Johann Auer, with whom I would meet up again in Regensburg, had been teaching in Bonn since 1950. Ludwig Hödl had come with me to Bonn as second specialist in the area of dogma. He was a great expert in the unprinted sources of medieval theology, and his mastery was rightly admired by the Schmaus school.

Across the faculties, too, friendships soon began to form that were important for my own development. I will mention only the Indologist Paul Hacker, whose universal talent I could only admire. He had trained as a specialist in Slavic studies, was a master of Indian languages (Indians came to him to study Sanskrit and Hindi), but was also unusually accomplished in Latin and Greek. Since in Bonn the history of religion was also taught within the general area of fundamental theology, the friendship that soon developed between us was particularly profitable to me. His studies in the history of religion were significant because of the high level of their subtle linguistic analysis as well as because of their penetration of the subject matter.

When I met him, Hacker was a practicing Lutheran but also a man who was always searching. His search had led him to Indology, but his explorations into the intellectual and spiritual universe of India had brought him back again to Christianity. Now he was plunging deep into the works of Luther as well as those of the Church Fathers. His passionate temperament knew no bounds, and so, for example, he would spend whole nights with one or more bottles of red wine in conversation with the Fathers or Luther. His road then led him into the Catholic Church, belonging at first to the faction critical of Rome. Later on he became more and more critical of the Council and inveighed especially against Karl Rahner's theology with a vehemence that, although quite in keeping with his volcanic temperament, nevertheless was not apt to win a hearing for his arguments. Thus, too, his book on Luther, the fruit of many years of inner struggle, was unfortunately brushed aside as the work of an outsider and a dilettante—neither of which he really was; the precision of his textual analyses remained unsurpassable to the end. I will here jump ahead a little to say that Hacker went to Münster shortly after I did, and there our exchanges became even deeper since now they no longer had to do so much with Indology (as at Bonn) but rather with his own theological inquiry. It was inevitable that such a friendship would include all kinds of tensions, but my gratitude to him remains unchanged because, both in the realm of theology and in that of the history of religion, I am much in his debt. The furious pace of his work habits burned him out too early. His work is hardly taken into account nowadays, but I am convinced that some day it will be rediscovered, and then it will still have much to say.

But now back to Bonn. I have wonderful memories of that first semester as one ongoing honeymoon. Along the way I had moved into pleasant living quarters in Bad Godesberg, which had not yet been joined to Bonn. Among the neighbors I had in this house, one in particular, the late Arno Esch, a specialist in English literature, became my friend. Right in the midst of the joyful sense of fresh beginning that had been with me all these months, there was in August an ominous drum roll that came with unexpected force and harshness. In August I had already gone with my sister to our parents' new house in the Hofgasse in Traunstein, where Father and Mother along with our brother were awaiting us with great joy. In the summer of 1958 Father had had a mild stroke while carrying my sister's heavy typewriter to the repair shop on a very hot day. Unfortunately we thought the episode insignificant because he seemed to have recovered immediately. Father kept to his round of occupations as if nothing had happened. As a matter of fact, if anything, he exhibited great clarity and particular deference and kindness in his dealings with us. At Christmas he gave us gifts whose generosity was beyond belief. We sensed that he took this to be his last Christmas, and yet we could not believe it, because exteriorly there was nothing wrong with him. In the middle of August he experienced an acute indisposition, from which he recovered only very slowly. On Sunday, August 23, Mother invited him to take a walk to the old places where we had lived and enjoyed our friends. On this hot summer day they walked together for more than ten kilometers. On their way home, Mother noticed how fervently Father prayed when they made a brief visit to the church and how restless he was awaiting the return of the three of us, who had taken a ride to Tittmoning. During supper he went out and collapsed at the top of the steps. He had had a serious stroke, which took him from us after exactly two days of suffering. We were grateful that we were all able to stand around his bed and again show him our love, which he accepted with gratitude even though he could no longer speak. When I returned to Bonn after this experience, I sensed that the world was emptier for me and that a portion of my home had been transferred to the other world.

10

Beginning of the Council and Transfer to Münster

While my relationship with Cardinal Wendel, the archbishop of Munich, had not been wholly without complications, a very straightforward and even affectionate understanding developed at once between the archbishop of Cologne, Cardinal Frings, and me. This was due in part to the fact that his secretary, Hubert Luthe, now bishop of Essen, was a friend of mine from the years in Fürstenried, where I had had a friendly rapport with several other theology students from Cologne, for instance, Bishop Dick, the present auxiliary bishop. Meanwhile, John XXIII had announced the Second Vatican Council and thereby reanimated and, for many, intensified even to the point of euphoria the atmosphere of renewal and hope that had reigned in the Church and in theology since the end of the First World War despite the perils of the National Socialist era. Cardinal Frings heard a conference on the theology of the Council that I had been invited to give by the Catholic Academy of Bensberg, and afterward he involved me in a long dialogue that became the starting point of a collaboration that lasted for years. As a member of the Central Preparatory Commission, the Cardinal was sent the drafts of texts ("schemata") that were to be presented to the Council Fathers for their discussion and vote after the assembly had convened. He now began to send me these texts regularly in order to have my criticism and suggestions for improvement. Naturally I took exception to certain things, but I found no grounds for a radical rejection of what was being proposed, such as many demanded later on in the Council and actually managed to put through. It is true that the documents bore only weak traces of the biblical and patristic renewal of the last decades, so that they gave an impression of rigidity and narrowness through their excessive dependency on scholastic theology. In other words, they reflected more the thought of scholars than that of shepherds. But I must say that they had a solid foundation and had been carefully elaborated.

Finally the great hour for the Council arrived. Cardinal Frings took his secretary, Father Luthe, and me, as his theological adviser, to Rome. He worked things so that I was named a *peritus* (or official Council theologian) toward the end of the first session. I cannot and will not enter here into a detailed portrayal of those very special years, during which we lived in the cozy "Anima", the residence for German and Austrian priests near the Piazza Navona, cannot recount the many encounters that were now granted me—with great men like Henri de Lubac, Jean Daniélou, and Gérard Philips, to name only a few prominent names—cannot report on the meetings with bishops from all continents or on personal conversations with only a few of them. Nor does the theological and ecclesial drama of those years belong in these memoirs.

But the reader will allow me two exceptions. The first question was what the Council should begin with, what its proximate task ought to be. The Pope had given only a very wide-ranging description of his purpose in calling a council, and this left the Fathers with an almost unlimited freedom to give things concrete shape. The Pope's view basically amounted to this: The faith, while remaining the same in its contents, was to be proclaimed to our era in a new way, and, after a period of demarcations and defensive maneuvers, we were now no longer to condemn but to apply the "medicine of mercy". There was implicit agreement that the Church herself should be the main theme of the gathering, which would thus take up again and conclude the work of the First Vatican Council, which had been prematurely interrupted in 1870 by the Franco-Prussian War. Cardinals Montini and Suenens presented plans for a vast theological outline of the work of the Council, in which the theme of the Church was to be divided into the two questions "the interior life of the Church" and "the Church vis-à-vis the world". This second part of the theme would permit the great questions of the present to come to the fore under the perspective of the relationship between Church and "world".

The reform of the liturgy in the spirit of the liturgical movement was not a priority for the majority of the Fathers, and for many not even a consideration. Thus, for example, in his outline of themes after the beginning of the Council, Cardinal Montini—who as Paul VI would be the real pope of the Council—said quite clearly that he did not see the reform of the liturgy as a substantial task in the Council. The liturgy and its reform had, since the end of World War I, become a pressing question only in France and Germany, and indeed above all from the perspective of the purest possible restoration of the ancient Roman liturgy, to which belonged the active involvement of the people in the liturgical event. These two countries, which at that time enjoyed theological leadership in the Church (and we must of course add Belgium and the Netherlands), had during the preparation phase succeeded in putting through a schema on the sacred liturgy, which quite naturally found its place in the general theme of the Church. The fact that this text became the first subject for the Council's discussions really had nothing to do with the majority of the Fathers having an intense interest in the liturgical question. Quite simply, no great disagreements were expected in this area, and the undertaking was viewed as a kind of practical exercise to learn and test the method of conciliar work. It would not have occurred to any of the Fathers to see in this text a "revolution" signifying the "end of the Middle Ages", as some theologians felt they should interpret it subsequently. The work was seen as a continuation of the reforms introduced by Pius X and carried on carefully but resolutely by Pius XII. General expressions such as "the liturgical books should be revised as soon as possible" (no. 25) were understood in this sense: as the uninterrupted continuation of that development which had always been there and which, since Popes Pius X and Pius XII, had received a definite profile from the rediscovery of the classical Roman liturgical traditions, which was, of course, to overcome certain tendencies of Baroque liturgy and nineteenth-century devotional piety and to promote a new humble and sober centering of the authentic mystery of Christ's presence in his Church. In this context it is not surprising that the "model Mass" now proposed, which was supposed to (and in fact did) take the place of the traditional *Ordo missae,* was in 1967 rejected by the majority of the Fathers who had been called together to a special synod on the matter. Some publications now tell us that some liturgists (or perhaps many?) who were working as advisers had had more far-reaching intentions from the outset. Their wishes would surely not have received the approval of the Fathers. Nor were such wishes expressed in any way in the text of the Council, although one can subsequently read them into some general statements.

The debate on the liturgy had taken place calmly and without serious tension. A dramatic controversy, however, did begin when the document on "The Sources of Revelation" was presented for discussion. By "sources of revelation", what was meant was Scripture and tradition; their relationship to one another and to the Magisterium had been dealt with solidly in the forms of post-Tridentine scholasticism according to the custom of the textbooks then in use. In the meantime, the historical-critical method of biblical interpretation had made itself at home in Catholic theology. By its very nature, this method has no patience with any restrictions imposed by an authoritative Magisterium; it can recognize no authority but that of the historical argument. From its perspective, the concept of "tradition" had itself become questionable, since this method will not allow for an oral tradition running alongside Scripture and reaching back to the apostles—and hence offering another source of historical knowledge besides the Bible. This impasse is indeed what had made the dispute on the dogma of Mary's bodily Assumption into heaven so difficult and insoluble.

Thus, with this text, the whole problem of modern biblical interpretation was up for debate and, beyond it, also the fundamental question of the relationship between history and spirit [*Geist*] within the context of faith. The concrete form of the debate was determined by an alleged historical discovery that the Tübingen dogma specialist J. R. Geiselmann believed he had made in the 1950s. In the Acts of the Council of Trent he had found that the initial formulation suggested for the decree issued at that time had stated that revelation was contained "partially in Scripture and partially in tradition". The definitive text, however, avoided this "partially/ partially", replacing it with an "and": in other words, Scripture and tradition *together* communicate revelation to us. From this, Geiselmann concluded that Trent had wanted to teach that there can be no distribution of the contents of faith into Scripture, on the one hand, and tradition, on the other, but rather that both Scripture and tradition, each on its own, contain the whole of revelation, hence that each is complete in itself. At this point what interested people was not the alleged or real completeness of tradition; the interesting thing was the announcement that, according to Trent, Scripture contains the deposit of faith whole and entire. There was talk of the "material completeness" of the Bible in matters of faith. This catchword, which was immediately on everybody's lips and was regarded as a great new realization, just as quickly became detached from its point of departure in the interpretation of the Tridentine decree. It was now asserted that the inevitable consequence of this realization was that the Church could not teach anything that was not expressly contained in Scripture, since Scripture was complete in matters of faith. And, since the interpretation of Scripture was identified with the historical-critical method, this meant that nothing could be taught by the Church that could not pass the scrutiny of the historical-critical method. With this Luther's *sola scriptura* ("Scripture alone"), which had been the main focus in Trent, was completely overshadowed. This new theory, in fact, meant that exegesis now had to become the highest authority in the Church; and since, by the very nature of human reason and historical work, no agreement among interpreters can be expected in the case of such difficult texts (since here acknowledged or unacknowledged prejudices are always at work), all of this meant that faith had to retreat into the region of the indeterminate and continually changing that characterizes historical or would-be historical hypotheses. In other words, believing now amounted to having opinions and was in need of continual revision. The Council, naturally, had to oppose a theory developed in this manner; but the catchword "material completeness", along with all its consequences, now remained in the Church's public awareness much more firmly than the Council's actual final document. The drama of the postconciliar era has been largely determined by this catchword and its logical consequences.

I had personally become acquainted with Geiselmann's thesis early in 1956 at the Königstein Congress of systematic theologians already mentioned. It was here that this scholar from Tübingen first proposed his alleged discovery (which, incidentally, he did not himself extend to all the consequences just described, something that developed only with the propaganda surrounding the Council). At first I too was fascinated, but soon I came to see that the great theme of Scripture and tradition could not be solved in so simple a manner. I then undertook a thorough study of the Acts of Trent and came to see that the redactional change that Geiselmann had made the main point was only an insignificant aspect of the Fathers' efforts, which searched much more deeply and extensively into the fundamental question of how revelation could be contained, first, in human words and, finally, in written words. In this I was helped by the knowledge I had gained while studying Bonaventure's concept of revelation. I found that the basic direction taken by the Fathers of Trent in their conception of revelation had essentially remained the same as in the High Middle Ages. On the basis of these principles, which I naturally cannot develop at any greater length here, my objections to the proposed conciliar schema were of a very different kind from either Geiselmann's theses or the cruder versions of them that circulated in the Council's increasingly heated atmosphere.

But I would at least like to sketch the essence of my thoughts on the matter. Revelation, which is to say, God's approach to man, is always greater than what can be contained in human words, greater even than the words of Scripture. As I have already said in connection with my work on Bonaventure, both in the Middle Ages and at Trent it would have been impossible to refer to Scripture simply as "revelation", as is the normal linguistic usage today. Scripture is the essential witness of revelation, but revelation is something alive, something greater and *more:* proper to it is the fact that it *arrives* and *is perceived*—otherwise it could not have become revelation. Revelation is not a meteor fallen to earth that now lies around somewhere as a rock mass from which rock samples can be taken and submitted to laboratory analysis. Revelation has instruments; but it is not separable from the living God, and it always requires a living person to whom it is communicated. Its goal is always to gather and unite men, and this is why the Church is a necessary aspect of revelation. If, however, revelation is more than Scripture, if it transcends Scripture, then the "rock analysis"—which is to say, the historical-critical method—cannot be the last word concerning revelation; rather, the living organism of the faith of all ages is then an intrinsic part of revelation. And what we call "tradition" is precisely that part of revelation that goes above and beyond Scripture and cannot be comprehended within a code of formulas. In the general atmosphere dominant in 1962, which had taken over Geiselmann's theses in the form I have described, it was impossible for me to explain the perspective I had gained from the sources, a perspective, moreover, that had already been misunderstood in 1956. My position was simply aligned with the general opposition to the official schema and considered to be one more vote in favor of Geiselmann.

At the request of Cardinal Frings, I wrote up at that time a brief schema in which I attempted to express my viewpoint. I had occasion to read my text, with Cardinal Frings present, to a number of highly regarded cardinals, who found it interesting but naturally neither wanted to, nor could at that moment, give any judgment concerning it. My small effort had been composed in great haste and so naturally could not in any way compete in solidity and thoroughness with the official schema, which had been elaborated in a long process and had gone through many revisions by competent scholars. It was clear that the text had to be reworked and deepened. For this other eyes and hands were needed. Thus, it was agreed that Karl Rahner and I together would produce a second, more developed version. This second text, much more Rahner's work than my own, was then distributed among the Fathers and evoked some rather bitter reactions. As we worked together, it became obvious to me that, despite our agreement in many desires and conclusions, Rahner and I lived on two different theological planets. In questions such as liturgical reform, the new place of exegesis in the Church and in theology, and in many other areas, he stood for the same things as I did, but for entirely different reasons. Despite his early reading of the Fathers, his theology was totally conditioned by the tradition of Suarezian scholasticism and its new reception in the light of German idealism and of Heidegger. His was a speculative and philosophical theology in which Scripture and the Fathers in the end did not play an important role and in which the historical dimension was really of little significance. For my part, my whole intellectual formation had been shaped by Scripture and the Fathers and profoundly historical thinking. The great difference between the Munich school, in which I had been trained, and Rahner's became clear to me during those days, even though it still took a while for our parting of ways to become outwardly visible.

It now became clear that Rahner's schema could not be accepted, but the official text, too, was rejected by a narrow margin of votes. The theme, therefore, had to be postponed. The Constitution on Divine Revelation could be completed only in the final period of the Council after some very complex debates, but the final product was one of the outstanding texts of the Council and one that has yet to be truly received. Practically the only thing that had any effect was what trickled down into popular opinion as the allegedly new viewpoint of the Fathers. We still have before us the task of communicating what the Council actually said to the Church at large and, beyond that, of developing its implications. In the meantime I had to make a difficult personal decision. The great dogma specialist from Münster, Hermann Volk, who despite the difference in our ages had become my friend, had been made bishop of Mainz in 1962. Now I was being invited to take his chair. I loved the Rhineland, and I loved my students and my work at the University of Bonn; because of Cardinal Frings I was even more committed to this work. But Bishop Volk was pressuring me, and friends advised me very emphatically that dogma was the correct road for me because it would open up a much wider sphere of influence than fundamental theology. They also argued that my formation in Scripture and the Fathers could be applied much more effectively in the area of dogma. Such an apparently simple decision nevertheless became difficult, and after much vacillation I decided to decline the Münster offer. This should have been the final word on the matter; but a splinter had remained in me that now began to hurt as I ran into considerable opposition within our tension-filled faculty in Bonn in connection with two doctoral dissertations. Such opposition would probably result in the failing of the two young scholars in question. I remembered the drama of my own *habilitation* and saw in Münster the way Providence was pointing out to me so that I could help these two candidates. That became even clearer when I realized that similar difficulties were also likely in other cases and that I had no reason to fear the same thing in Münster given the circumstances there. Together with the arguments concerning my greater involvement in dogma, which I had previously discounted, these other reasons now amounted to a force to which I yielded. Of course, I had discussed all these things with Cardinal Frings and can even now feel only gratitude for his fatherly understanding and personal generosity. Thus, in the summer of 1963 I took up my post lecturing in Münster, where both the personal and the material situation granted me was generous. My reception by colleagues in the faculty was very warm, and conditions could hardly have been more favorable. But I must admit that I retained a certain nostalgia for Bonn, the city on the river, for its cheerfulness and intellectual dynamism.

Nineteen sixty-three brought yet another deep wound to my life. Already since January my brother had noticed that Mother was eating less and less. In mid-August her physician announced to us with sad certainty that she had cancer of the stomach, which would follow its course quickly and relentlessly. With what was left of her energies she kept house for my brother until the end of October, even though she was already reduced to skin and bones. Then one day she collapsed in a shop, and then was never again able to leave her sickbed. Our experience with her now was very similar to what we had lived with Father. Her goodness became even purer and more radiant and continued to shine unchanged even through the weeks of increasing pain. On the day after Gaudete Sunday, December 16, 1963, she closed her eyes forever, but the radiance of her goodness has remained, and for me it has become more and more a confirmation of the faith by which she had allowed herself to be formed. I know of no more convincing proof for the faith than precisely the pure and unalloyed humanity that the faith allowed to mature in my parents and in so many other persons I have had the privilege to encounter.

11

Münster and Tübingen

In February 1964, almost immediately after our dear mother's death, my brother succeeded Theobald Schrems as choir director of Regensburg Cathedral and thus also director of the world-famous Regensburger Domspatzen. This meant that the Traunstein idyll had come to an end once and for all, and Regensburg, the old imperial city on the Danube, until now rather at the periphery of our lives, became for us a common point of reference. We would meet in Regensburg for vacation, and gradually we began to feel at home here. Meanwhile the Council went on, and I lived and worked dividing my time between Münster and Rome. General interest in theology, which had already been great in Germany, now began to grow under the pressure of frequently exciting news about discussions among the Fathers. Now and then, on returning from Rome, I found the mood in the Church and among theologians to be quite agitated. The impression grew steadily that nothing was now stable in the Church, that everything was open to revision. More and more the Council appeared to be like a great Church parliament that could change everything and reshape everything according to its own desires. Very clearly resentment was growing against Rome and against the Curia, which appeared to be the real enemy of everything that was new and progressive. The disputes at the Council were more and more portrayed according to the party model of modern parliamentarism. When information was presented in this way, the person receiving it saw himself compelled to take sides with one of the parties. Even though in Germany by and large there was almost undivided support for the forces of renewal, divisions nevertheless began gradually to mark the ecclesial landscape of my homeland that mimicked what was happening in the Council. Something else, however, with deeper implications, was also happening. If the bishops in Rome could change the faith (as it appeared they could), why only the bishops? In any event, the faith could be changed—or so it now appeared, in contrast to everything we had previously thought. The faith no longer seemed exempt from human decision making but rather was now apparently determined by it. And we knew that the bishops had learned from theologians the new things they were now proposing. For believers, it was a remarkable phenomenon that their bishops seemed to show a different face in Rome from the one they wore at home. Shepherds who had been considered strict conservatives suddenly appeared to be spokesmen for progressivism. But were they doing this all on their own? The role that theologians had assumed at the Council was creating ever more clearly a new confidence among scholars, who now understood themselves to be the truly knowledgeable experts in the faith and therefore no longer subordinate to the shepherds. For, how could the bishops in the exercise of their teaching office preside over theologians when they, the bishops, received their insights only from specialists and thus were dependent on the guidance of scholars? In his time, Luther had exchanged his priestly robes for the scholar's gown, in order to show that the Scripture scholars in the Church were the ones who had to make the decisions. This radical change was then somewhat stifled by the normative character of the Creed. It was the Creed that provided the standard also for scholarly science. But now in the Catholic Church all of this—at least in the popular consciousness—was up once again for revision, and even the Creed no longer appeared untouchable but seemed rather subject to the control of scholars. Behind this tendency to dominance by specialists one could already detect something else: the idea of an ecclesial sovereignty of the people in which the people itself determines what it wants to understand by Church, since "Church" already seemed very clearly defined as "People of God". The idea of the "Church from below", the "Church of the People", which then became the goal of reform particularly in the context of liberation theology, was thus heralded.

When I came home after the Council's first session, I had been filled with the joyful feeling, dominant everywhere, of an important new beginning. Now I became deeply troubled by the change in ecclesial climate that was becoming ever more evident. In a presentation at the University of Münster on true and false renewal of the Church, I tried to sound a first warning signal, but few if any noticed. I then became more emphatic at the Bamberg Catholic Congress of 1966, so much so that Cardinal Döpfner expressed surprise at the "conservative streak" he thought he detected. But a personal change again stood before me. In Münster, as I have said, I had been well received and esteemed among my colleagues; I had eager and encouraging audiences and a professional situation that could hardly be surpassed. I began to love this beautiful and noble city more and more. And yet there was one negative aspect: the great distance from my native Bavaria, a land with which I have deep inner bonds. I was being drawn to the south. Hence, the temptation was irresistible when the University of Tübingen, which had already offered me the chair in fundamental theology in 1959, now invited me to accept a newly created second chair in dogma. Hans Küng had vigorously supported such an appointment and obtained the agreement of his colleagues. I had met him in 1957 at a congress of dogmatic theologians in Innsbruck, just as I had completed my review of his doctoral work on Karl Barth. I had many questions to ask of this book because, although its theological style was not my own, I had read it with pleasure and gained respect for its author, whose winning openness and straightforwardness I quite liked. A good personal relationship was thus established, even if soon after my review of his book a rather serious argument began between us about the theology of the Council. But both of us regarded this as one of the legitimate differences in theological position that are necessary for the fruitful development of thought, and we did not feel that our personal liking for one another or our ability to collaborate was in any way compromised by such differences.

As things continued to develop both within theology and in the Church, I sensed that our ways would diverge even farther, and yet I continued to think that the fundamental consensus to be expected among Catholic theologians would remained untouched. I must say that at that point I felt closer to Küng's work than to that of J. B. Metz, who on my recommendation had been invited to Münster to occupy the chair in fundamental theology. I always found discussion with him to be very stimulating, but when he started taking a turn toward political theology, I saw a conflict emerging that could go deep indeed. In any event, I decided to accept the post in Tübingen. The south beckoned, but also the great history of theology at this Swabian university, where interesting encounters with important Lutheran theologians were also to be expected.

My work as lecturer began at Tübingen in the summer semester of 1966, with my health in rather bad condition due to the stress of the conciliar period, the closing of the Council, and the need to commute initially back and forth between Münster and Tübingen. The magic of this small Swabian town soon worked its spell on me; at the same time my accommodations were not exactly luxurious. Everything seemed narrow and sparse in comparison to the generous scale of what I had had in Münster, and so I was a little disappointed. All of the faculty were first-rate but also much given to conflict, and this was something I was no longer used to. But I must say that I was on good terms with all my colleagues there. The "signs of the times" that I had begun to detect in Münster were now becoming more obviously dramatic. At first Rudolf Bultmann's theology still dominated the theological climate, in the particular variation given to it by Ernst Käsemann. My lectures on Christology in the winter semester of 1966–1967 focused wholly on this discussion. In 1967 we were still able to celebrate brilliantly the 150th anniversary of the creation of the Faculty for Catholic Theology at Tübingen; but this was the last celebration in the old style. At almost a moment's notice, there was a change in the ideological "paradigm" by which the students and a part of the teachers thought. While until now Bultmann's theology and Heidegger's philosophy had determined the frame of reference for thinking, almost overnight the existentialist model collapsed and was replaced by the Marxist. Ernst Bloch was now teaching in Tübingen and made Heidegger contemptible for being petty bourgeois. At about the same time as I arrived, Jürgen Moltmann came to the Faculty for Lutheran Theology. In his fascinating book *A Theology of Hope,* Moltmann gives a wholly new and different conception of theology from Bloch's perspective.

Existentialism fell apart, and the Marxist revolution kindled the whole university with its fervor, shaking it to its very foundations. A few years before, one could still have expected the theological faculties to represent a bulwark against the Marxist temptation. Now the opposite was the case: they became its real ideological center. The admission of existentialism into theology, as accomplished by Bultmann, was not without dangers for theology. As I have said, in my Christology I had attempted to fight against the existentialist reduction, especially in the doctrine about God, which is one of the first things I had to lecture on. Here and there I had even tried to introduce counterbalances from Marxist thought, which, in its Jewish-messianic roots, still also preserved biblical motifs. But the destruction of theology that was now occurring (through its politicization as conceived by Marxist messianism) was incomparably more radical precisely because it took biblical hope as its basis but inverted it by keeping the religious ardor but eliminating God and replacing him with the political activity of man. Hope remains, but the party takes the place of God, and, along with the party, a totalitarianism that practices an atheistic sort of adoration ready to sacrifice all humanness to its false god. I myself have seen the frightful face of this atheistic piety unveiled, its psychological terror, the abandon with which every moral consideration could be thrown overboard as a bourgeois residue when the ideological goal was at stake. All of this is alarming enough in itself; but it becomes an unrelenting challenge to the theologian when the ideology is presented in the name of the faith and the Church is used as its instrument. The blasphemous manner in which the Cross now came to be despised as a sign of sadomasochism, the hypocrisy with which some still passed themselves off as believers when this was useful, in order not to jeopardize the instruments that were to serve their own private ends: all of this could and should not be made to look harmless or regarded as just another academic quarrel. Since, at the height of these debates, I was dean of my faculty, a member of the Greater and Lesser Academic Senate, and a member also of the commission in charge of designing a new constitution for the university, I experienced all these things at very close range indeed.

There naturally continued to be many quite ordinary theology students as well. It was actually a small circle of functionaries who drove developments in the direction I have described. But it was this circle who determined the reigning climate. I never had difficulties with students. On the contrary, I was able to continue speaking to a lecture hall full of attentive listeners. I would have considered it a betrayal, however, to withdraw to the tranquillity of my lecture hall and leave everything else to the others. In the Lutheran Theological Faculty the situation was much more dramatic than in ours. Yet we were sitting in the same boat. At this conjuncture I joined two Lutheran theologians in trying to plan a common course of action; they were the patristic scholar Ulrich Wickert and the missionologist Wolfgang Beyerhaus. We saw that the confessional controversies we had previously engaged in were small indeed in the face of the challenge we now confronted, which put us in a position of having, together, to bear witness to our common faith in the living God and in Christ, the incarnate Word. My friendship with these two colleagues remains one of the most precious gifts given me by my years in Tübingen. Wickert, by the way, soon made a decision similar to mine. He had no inclination to live in a battle zone and so accepted an offer from the Kirchliche Hochschule in Berlin, where he could carry on with his theological work in a less agitated environment. Beyerhaus had more of a fighting nature than the two of us, and thus he became the spokesman for the Lutherans, going through his battles against this basic background.

Before I proceed to the next stage of my life's road, perhaps I should say again that, despite all these events, much normal and fruitful work could still be accomplished. Since Hans Küng was responsible in 1967 for the main series of lectures in dogma, I was finally free to realize a project I had been quietly pondering for ten years. I ventured to prepare a lecture series for students of all faculties under the title "Introduction to Christianity". Out of these lectures came a book, which has been translated into seventeen languages and has had a great number of editions, and not just in Germany. It is still read. I was and am very conscious of its many flaws; but through it I was able to open a door for many, and this brings me satisfaction and gives me an occasion to thank Tübingen, since these lectures came to be in its ambiance.

12

The Regensburg Years

Meanwhile, in 1967, a plan of very long standing finally became a reality. The Free State of Bavaria erected its fourth university in the city of Regensburg. From the very beginning there had been intentions to appoint me to the chair for dogma, but I had refused. In the first place, I belonged to the committee for academic appointments established by the Ministry and therefore could not engage in any conflict of interests. At the same time, moreover, I was tired of moving from place to place and hoped to be able finally to enter a period of quiet work in Tübingen. Johann Auer accepted the post in my place. He was a former colleague of mine in Bonn and a native of Regensburg and someone I already knew from my student days in Munich. Thus he returned to his city of birth to spend many fruitful years there. But I was again approached when, in late 1968 or early 1969, a second chair for dogma was established in Regensburg. I was still dean, but the exhausting controversies I experienced during academic meetings had changed my attitude. I indicated my willingness. So, in 1969, I received a formal invitation to go to Regensburg, which I accepted, because, like Wickert, I wanted to develop my theology further in a less agitated environment and also because I did not want to be always forced into the contra position. The fact that my brother was working in Regensburg, and that thus the family could be together in one place, was another reason in favor of the new change. But it was clear to me that this change very definitely had to be the last.

The beginning was not easy. The university buildings were still being constructed, and a part of our work took place in the old building of the Theological College, which had been the monastery of the Dominicans in Regensburg. With its cloister, winding corridors, and the adjoining Gothic Dominican church, it offered a very special atmosphere. The students first had to get used to university life, and the individual faculties developed their profile only little by little. The waves of Marxist revolt naturally pounded against our young Alma Mater too. Particularly within the circle of assistant professors there were many very determined leftists. But the university began to take shape quite quickly, and we succeeded in drawing renowned professors to the Danube, with the result that friendships soon began to form across the different faculties, especially law, philosophy, and natural science. With great rapidity students began to arrive from outside Bavaria and Germany, and my own circle of doctoral candidates became even more international and varied with respect to differences in talents and intellectual positions. Thus, we soon had once again the exchange of ideas so desirable at a university and so important for me in my work. There was no lack of controversies, but we had the fundamental respect for one another that is so important for fruitful work.

Right at the beginning of my years in Regensburg came a series of decisive events. The first was my appointment to the International Papal Theological Commission. Pope Paul VI had established it at the insistence of bishops and cardinals who could for the most part be numbered within the so-called progressive wing of the Council Fathers. Just as the synod of bishops was supposed to keep the conciliar method alive and give the bishops of the universal Church a participation in central decisions, so too this Commission was intended to implement the new function that the Council had assigned theologians and ensure that modern theological developments entered from the outset into the decision-making process of bishops and of the Holy See itself. The Council had given the impression that the theology deriving from papal authorities and the theology developing in the different local Churches were in divergence from one another, and the Commission was to see that such a split disappeared. Some also thought that the Theological Commission should create a counterweight to the Congregation for the Doctrine of the Faith, or at least provide this Congregation with a new and wholly different "brain trust". Many, indeed, hoped that the new panel of theologians would guarantee something like constant revolution. Accordingly, there was considerable tension within the Commission, which had been appointed for a first period of five years. Almost all of its members had taken part in the Council, and, within the theological configuration that then obtained, they could all be said to have a progressive orientation. And so the first interesting thing was to see how the individual members of this Commission had received the experiences of the postconciliar period and had defined their own position within them. For me it was very encouraging to see that many of them judged the present situation and our tasks within it in the same way I did. Henri de Lubac, who had suffered so much under the narrowness of the neoscholastic regime, showed himself to be a decided fighter against the fundamental threat to the faith that now was changing all previous theological positions. Something similar may be said of Philippe Delhaye. Jorge Medina, a theologian from

Chile the same age as myself, saw the situation as I did. New friends were arriving: M.-J. Le Guillou, a great expert in Orthodox theology, was fighting for the theology of the Fathers against the dissolution of the faith into political moralism. A mind with a very special character was that of Louis Bouyer, a convert with extraordinary knowledge of the Fathers, the history of the liturgy, and biblical and Jewish traditions.

Then came the great figure of Hans Urs von Balthasar. I first met him in Bonn on an occasion when he had invited a small group to discuss the "model of the Christian open to the world" proposed by Alfons Auer, a moral theologian who was then in Würzburg and was later to go to Tübingen. Balthasar saw this model as a total misunderstanding of the Bible, as a misunderstanding, too, of his own position concerning the "razing of the bastions", and he hoped that a dialogue within a small circle could put an end in a timely fashion to such mistaken developments. Unfortunately, Auer himself did not come, and so there could be no direct dialogue; but meeting Balthasar was for me the beginning of a lifelong friendship I can only be thankful for. Never again have I found anyone with such a comprehensive theological and humanistic education as Balthasar and de Lubac, and I cannot even begin to say how much I owe to my encounter with them. In keeping with his conciliatory nature, Congar always tried to mediate between opposites, and with this patient openness he surely fulfilled an important mission. He was a man of enormous diligence and a discipline in work that sickness itself could not restrain. Rahner, on the other hand, for the most part allowed himself to be "sworn in" according to the progressive slogans, and allowed himself as well to be pushed into adventuresome political positions difficult to reconcile with his own transcendental philosophy.

The debates over what we as theologians were bound to do in this critical hour were animated in the extreme, and they also required all the physical energy at one's disposal. Rahner and Feiner, the Swiss ecumenist, finally left the Commission because, in their opinion, it was worthless since the majority of its members was not ready to subscribe to radical theses.

Balthasar, who had not been invited to the Council and who could judge the newly emerging situation with great acumen, was seeking for new solutions to divert theology from the partisanship toward which it was more and more tending. His project was to gather together all those who did not want to do theology on the basis of the pre-set goals of ecclesial politics but who were intent on developing theology rigorously on the basis of its own proper sources and methods. This is how the idea was born to start an international journal whose work would both be done out of the heart of communion in sacrament and faith and also lead to its enhancement. We often discussed this idea with de Lubac, Bouyer, Le Guillou, and Medina. At first it seemed that the project could be realized in Germany and France. But then difficulties emerged in France, especially because Le Guillou fell ill. In the meantime, Balthasar had met in Milan the founder of the Communion and Liberation Movement, Luigi Giussani, and his young people, who were so full of promise. And so the journal first saw the light in Germany and Italy, with a special character in each case. For it was our conviction that this publication was not to be exclusively theological. Since the crisis in theology had emerged out of a crisis in culture and, indeed, out of a cultural revolution, the journal had to address the cultural domain, too, and had to be edited in collaboration with lay persons of high cultural competence. Since cultures are very different from country to country, the review had to take this into account and have something like a "federalist" character.

In Germany we won the support of Karl Lehmann, a dogmatic theologian then in Freiburg who is now bishop of Mainz. For a publisher we found Franz Greiner, the last publisher of *Hochland,* the once famous Catholic cultural journal. To our number were added: Hans Maier, then Bavarian minister of culture, whom, as a young political scientist at the University of Munich, I had met during my Tübingen years; the psychologist A. Görres; and O. B. Roegele, professor of journalism in Munich and founder of the *Rheinischer Merkur.* Since then, *Communio* has come out in sixteen languages, becoming an important instrument for theological and cultural discussion, even if it still has not totally achieved what we first had in mind. In any case, it has for a long time remained too academic, and we have not succeeded in intervening in the contemporary debate in a sufficiently concrete and timely manner. Nevertheless, the publication performs an important service, and the years of collaboration with the community of editors widened my horizons and taught me many things.

Alongside the two significant events of the International Theological Commission and the journal *Communio,* I must now mention a more modest experience. I was pursued by the thought that Romano Guardini could never have attained within the university alone the great sphere of influence that he exercised in the 1920s and 1930s. Through an independent group of young people at Rothenfels Castle, he had created a spiritual and intellectual center that then raised his work at the university above the merely academic. Something similar now had to be attempted again, even if in a much more modest form, considering the changed cultural situation. Together with Baroness von

Stockhausen of Westphalia, Dr. Lehmann-Dronke, one of my students, had at his disposal in the region of Lake Constance an old farming estate that had been remodeled into a house of studies, which was now being offered for just such an endeavor as I had in mind. Here, every year from 1970 to 1977, together with the great exegete Heinrich Schlier, a Catholic convert, I offered a one-week course during vacation time. The cheerful and relaxed atmosphere, along with the sharing of simple everyday activities, made both our theological dialogue and our communal prayer very fruitful. I had met Schlier during my years in Bonn, and now I was able to profit a great deal from his manner of interpreting Scripture, at once philologically precise and spiritually profound. He was one of the truly noble figures of twentieth-century theology, deeply indebted to Heidegger and Bultmann (he had been the latter's student) and yet going far beyond them both. I am certain that his work, largely forgotten at present, will be rediscovered.

The second great event at the beginning of my years in Regensburg was the publication of the Missal of Paul VI, which was accompanied by the almost total prohibition, after a transitional phase of only half a year, of using the missal we had had until then. I welcomed the fact that now we had a binding liturgical text after a period of experimentation that had often deformed the liturgy. But I was dismayed by the prohibition of the old missal, since nothing of the sort had ever happened in the entire history of the liturgy. The impression was even given that what was happening was quite normal. The previous missal had been created by Pius V in 1570 in connection with the Council of Trent; and so it was quite normal that, after four hundred years and a new council, a new pope would present us with a new missal. But the historical truth of the matter is different.

Pius V had simply ordered a reworking of the *Missale Romanum* then being used, which is the normal thing as history develops over the course of centuries. Many of his successors had likewise reworked this missal again, but without ever setting one missal against another. It was a continual process of growth and purification in which continuity was never destroyed. There is no such thing as a "Missal of Pius V", created by Pius V himself. There is only the reworking done by Pius V as one phase in a long history of growth. The new feature that came to the fore after the Council of Trent was of a different nature. The irruption of the Reformation had above all taken the concrete form of liturgical "reforms". It was not just a matter of there being a Catholic Church and a Protestant Church alongside one another. The split in the Church occurred almost imperceptibly and found its most visible and historically most incisive manifestation in the changes of the liturgy. These changes, in turn, took very different forms at the local level, so that here, too, one frequently could not ascertain the boundary between what was still Catholic and what was no longer Catholic.

In this confusing situation, which had become possible by the failure to produce unified liturgical legislation and by the existing liturgical pluralism inherited from the Middle Ages, the pope decided that now the *Missale Romanum*—the missal of the city of Rome—was to be introduced as reliably Catholic in every place that could not demonstrate its liturgy to be at least two hundred years old. Wherever the existing liturgy was that old, it could be preserved because its Catholic character would then be assured. In this case we cannot speak of the prohibition of a previous missal that had formerly been approved as valid. The prohibition of the missal that was now decreed, a missal that had known continuous growth over the centuries, starting with the sacramentaries of the ancient Church, introduced a breach into the history of the liturgy whose consequences could only be tragic. It was reasonable and right of the Council to order a revision of the missal such as had often taken place before and which this time had to be more thorough than before, above all because of the introduction of the vernacular.

But more than this now happened: the old building was demolished, and another was built, to be sure largely using materials from the previous one and even using the old building plans. There is no doubt that this new missal in many respects brought with it a real improvement and enrichment; but setting it as a new construction over against what had grown historically, forbidding the results of this historical growth, thereby makes the liturgy appear to be no longer a living development but the product of erudite work and juridical authority; this has caused us enormous harm. For then the impression had to emerge that liturgy is something "made", not something given in advance but something lying within our own power of decision. From this it also follows that we are not to recognize the scholars and the central authority alone as decision makers, but that in the end each and every "community" must provide itself with its own liturgy. When liturgy is self-made, however, then it can no longer give us what its proper gift should be: the encounter with the mystery that is not our own product but rather our origin and the source of our life. A renewal of liturgical awareness, a liturgical reconciliation that again recognizes the unity of the history of the liturgy and that understands Vatican II, not as a breach, but as a stage of development: these things are urgently needed for the life of the Church. I am convinced that the crisis in the Church that we are experiencing today is to a large extent due to the disintegration of the liturgy, which at times has even come to be conceived of *etsi Deus non daretur:* in that it is a matter of indifference whether or not God exists and whether or not he speaks to us and hears us. But when the community of faith, the worldwide unity of the Church and her history, and the mystery of the living Christ are no longer visible in the liturgy, where else, then, is the Church to become visible in her spiritual essence? Then the community is celebrating only itself, an activity that is utterly fruitless. And, because the ecclesial community cannot have its origin from itself but emerges as a unity only from the Lord, through faith, such circumstances will inexorably result in a disintegration into sectarian parties of all kinds—partisan opposition within a Church tearing herself apart. This is why we need a new Liturgical Movement, which will call to life the real heritage of the Second Vatican Council.

The Regensburg years, I must say, were a time of fruitful theological work for me. I was confronted with two big projects that, to be sure, were never realized because of my being named a bishop. After the great success of Father Häring's moral theology in one volume, the publisher behind this book, Wewel, now had the idea of producing a book of dogmatic theology of the same type. Karl Rahner was invited to be its author around 1957. Because of heavy commitments, Rahner turned down the project but recommended me. It was an undeserved honor, since I was then young and unknown. I knew the limits of my abilities, and so I made it a condition that I could look for a coauthor. My idea was approved, and I convinced Father Grillmeier to join me in the enterprise. At that time I worked diligently on the project, and my sister copied several hundred pages; but the Council stopped further attempts at writing, and after the Council it was impossible to return immediately to the task I had accepted. But now I was to have the time to do this.

Then a new difficulty arose. Professor Auer had just then begun to realize an old idea of his, which was to produce a dogmatic theology in a small, paperback format. Mostly at the urging of his publisher, Pustet, he asked me insistently to join him as coauthor. I informed him of my commitment to the project with Wewel, but in the end I yielded to his request and took over those parts in his work that Father Grillmeier was to write for the Wewel book on dogma. Hard feelings developed with Wewel, but these were later resolved. In any event, I was able to complete neither of the two projects. I succeeded only in writing the eschatology portion of Auer's dogmatics, something I still consider my most thorough work and the one I labored over most strenuously. After the decisive turning point of the Council, I first simply tried to conceive my whole dogmatics anew, going back again to the sources and keeping abreast of what was being produced. Thus, a vision of the whole gradually grew for me that was nourished by the various experiences and realizations I had encountered along my theological path. I rejoiced to be able to say something of my own, something new and yet completely within the faith of the Church; but apparently I was not called to do this. Just as I was beginning to get down to work, I was called to another task.

The feeling of acquiring a theological vision that was ever more clearly my own was the most wonderful experience of the Regensburg years. I had been able to build a small house with a garden that became a real home for my sister and me and to which my brother always liked to return. We were once again at home together. For my brother, too, these were blessed years. Performances of Schütz, Bach, Vivaldi, and Monteverdi received international prizes, and the millennial anniversary of the Regensburg Cathedral Choir was celebrated with great splendor in 1976. When on July

24, 1976, the news of the sudden death of the archbishop of Munich, Julius Cardinal Döpfner, was broadcast, all of us were shocked. Rumors at once began circulating that I was among the candidates to succeed him. I did not take them very seriously, because my limitations with regard to health were as well-known as my inability in matters of governance and administration. I knew I was called to the scholar's life and never considered anything else. Academic offices—I was now dean again and vice-president of the university—remained within the realm of functions that a professor must assume and were very far from the responsibilities of a bishop.

13

Archbishop of Munich and Freising

Thus, I still did not think it was anything serious when Del Mestri, the apostolic nuncio, visited me in Regensburg under some pretext. We chatted about insignificant matters, and then finally he pressed a letter into my hand, telling me to read it and think it over at home. It contained my appointment as archbishop of Munich and Freising. I was allowed to consult my confessor on the matter. So I went to Professor Auer, who had very realistic knowledge of my limitations, both theological and human. I surely expected him to advise me to decline. But to my great surprise he said without much reflection: "You must accept." I went back to the nuncio and again explained my reservations; but in the end, with him as my witness, I hesitantly wrote my acceptance on the stationery of the hotel where he was staying. The weeks before the consecration were difficult. Interiorly I was still very unsure, and in addition I had a huge burden of work that was nearly crushing me. And so it was in rather poor health that I approached the day of consecration. The day itself was extraordinarily beautiful—a radiant day in early summer, the vigil of Pentecost 1977. The cathedral in Munich, which was left rather sober by restorations after World War II, was splendidly decorated and filled with a joyous atmosphere that was irresistible. I experienced what a sacrament is—that what occurs in a sacrament is reality.

Then there was the prayer before the Pillar of Our Lady in the heart of the Bavarian capital, the encounter with so many people who were welcoming this unknown person with a heartfelt warmth and joy that could not possibly have had to do with me personally but that once again showed me what a sacrament is: I was being greeted as bishop, as bearer of the Mystery of Christ, even if the majority were not explicitly conscious of this. The joy of the day was something really different from approval of a particular person, whose qualifications still had to be demonstrated. It was joy over the fact that this office, this service, was again present in a person who does not act and live for himself but for Him and therefore for all.

This episcopal consecration brings me into the present period of my life. For the present is not a specific date but the Now of a human life. And this Now can be long or very short. For me, the Now of my life is still determined by what began in the cathedral in Munich that day with the laying on of hands for my consecration as bishop. This is why I cannot write any memoirs about it but can only attempt to fill in this Now.

What am I to say at the conclusion of this biographical sketch? As my episcopal motto I selected the phrase from the Third Letter of John, "Co-worker of the Truth". For one, it seemed to be the connection between my previous task as teacher and my new mission. Despite all the differences in modality, what is involved was and remains the same: to follow the truth, to be at its service. And, because in today's world the theme of truth has all but disappeared, because truth appears to be too great for man and yet everything falls apart if there is no truth, for these reasons this motto also seemed timely in the good sense of the word. For about a thousand years the coat of arms of the bishops of Freising has borne a crowned Moor, but no one is quite sure what it means. For me it is a sign of the universality of the Church, which knows no distinction of races or classes, since all of us "are one" in Christ (Gal 3:28).

I selected for myself two additional symbols. The first of these was the shell, which first of all is simply a sign of our pilgrimage, of our being on the road: "We have here no lasting city." But it also reminded me of the legend according to which one day Augustine, pondering the mystery of the Trinity, saw a child at the seashore playing with a shell, trying to put the water of the ocean into a little hole. Then he heard the words: This hole can no more contain the waters of the ocean than your intellect can comprehend the mystery of God. Thus, for me the shell points to my great master, Augustine, to my own theological work, and to the greatness of the mystery that extends farther than all our knowledge.

The second symbol was the bear, which I took from the legend of Corbinian, founder-bishop of Freising. The story has it that, on the way to Rome, a bear tore the saint's horse to pieces. Then Corbinian reprimanded the bear sternly for its crime and as punishment loaded on it the pack that the horse had been carrying. The bear had to haul the pack all the way to Rome, and only there was it released by the saint. The bear weighed down with the saint's burden reminded me of one of Saint Augustine's meditations on the Psalms. In verses 22 and 23 of Psalm 72 (73), he saw expressed both the burden and the hope of his life. What he finds in these verses and then comments is like a self-portrait, made before the face of God, and therefore not just a pious thought but an exegesis of his life and a light upon his road.

What Augustine writes in this connection became for me a portrayal of my own destiny. This psalm from the wisdom tradition shows the straits of faith that comes from the absence of earthly success. When you stand on the side of God, you do not necessarily stand on the side of success. Good fortune often seems to pamper precisely the cynics. How are we to understand this? The psalmist finds the answer by standing before God, in whose presence he grasps the ultimate insignificance of material wealth and success and recognizes what is truly necessary and what brings salvation. "Ut iumentum factus sum apud te et ego semper tecum." Modern translations render the passage like this: "When my heart was bewildered . . . , I was stupid and ignorant, I was like a dumb beast before you. And yet I am always with you." Augustine understood the word "beast" somewhat differently. The Latin word *iumentum* referred primarily to draft animals used for farmwork in the fields, and here he sees an image of himself under the burden of his episcopal service: "A draft animal am I before you, for you, and this is precisely how I abide with you." He had chosen the life of a scholar, but God had chosen to make him into a "draft animal"—a good, sturdy ox to pull God's cart in this world. How often did he protest vehemently against all the trifles that continually blocked his path and kept him from the great spiritual and intellectual work he knew to be his deepest calling! But this is where the psalm helps him avoid all bitterness: "Yes, indeed, I have become a draft animal, a beast of burden, an ox—and yet this is just the way in which I am with you, serving you, just the way in which you keep me in your hand." Just as the draft animal is closest to the farmer, doing his work for him, so is Augustine closest to God precisely through such humble service, completely within God's hand, completely his instrument. He could not be closer to his Lord or be more important to him. The laden bear that took the place of Saint Corbinian's horse, or rather donkey—the bear that became his donkey against its will: Is this not an image of what I should do and of what I am? "A beast of burden have I become for you, and this is just the way for me to remain wholly yours and always abide with you."

What else could I say in detail about my years as a bishop? It is said of Corbinian that, once in Rome, he again released the bear to its freedom. The legend is not concerned about whether it went up into the Abruzzi or returned to the Alps. In the meantime I have carried my load to Rome and have now been wandering the streets of the Eternal City for a long time. I do not know when I will be released, but one thing I do know: that the exclamation applies to me too: "I have become your donkey, and in just this way am I with you."